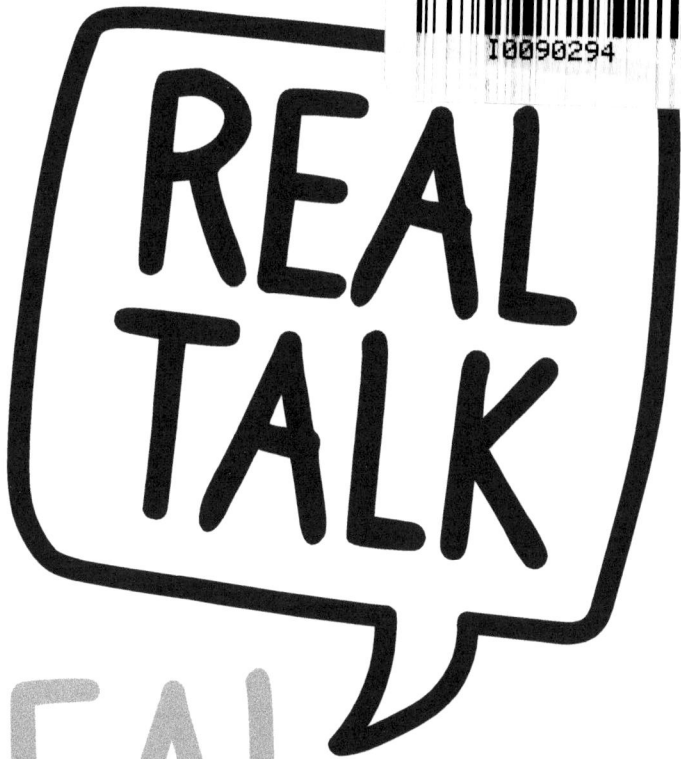

REAL TALK

REAL CHANGE

Life Strategies From A
Psychologist And Life Coach

REAL TALK

REAL CHANGE

Life Strategies From A
Psychologist And Life Coach

DR NATASHA DAVISON

First published in 2020 by Dean Publishing
PO Box 119
Mt. Macedon, Victoria, 3441
Australia
deanpublishing.com

DEAN PUBLISHING

Cataloguing-in-Publication Data
National Library of Australia
Title: Real Talk, Real Change — Life Strategies From A Psychologist And
Life Coach
Edition: 1st edn
ISBN: 978-1-925452-24-2
Category: Self-help/Psychology

DEDICATION

♡

*For my husband Alan and my daughter Madalyn, who have
taught me the true meaning of unconditional love.*

*For my angel babies Max and Nicholas, who taught me that
I was much stronger than I ever believed I was.*

*For my brave and amazing clients, past, current and future,
who courageously step into the unknown, share their lives
with me and trust me to be their guide. This is for you.*

CONTENTS

Author Disclaimer

This is more of a conversation than a book, or perhaps more accurately — it's a conversation within a book. I have deliberately made it this way for one reason only; I wanted this book to 'talk' to real people who want real change in their lives. That is the primary and only goal.

You will notice the lack of scientific references, data and research cited in this book. Don't be shocked. It was deliberate — it's not that kind of book. And though of course, my background and training is entrenched in theory, peer-reviewed papers and research, and I am a registered psychologist, and the tools and discussions used in my book are from well-established, evidence-based models, I have left out the referenced scientific data. Not because it's not awesome, because it is. But so we can simply sit down, maybe over a cuppa and I can talk directly to you, about *you*. Concentrate on what you want and what *your* goals and dreams are. What do you want out of life? How do you want life to be?

I wanted it to be simple. It's what I do when I work alongside my clients in sessions. I don't quote references and data in sessions and it's exactly what I didn't want to do here. So I have simply collated some helpful tools and strategies that I have personally used and learnt over the years and have seen work in the lives of my clients and put them into a 'book conversation'. As one client said to me, it's like 'a chat with Dr Nat.' And that's exactly how I intended it to be.

Warning: I do swear, I do personally share, and I don't cite research or peer-viewed publications. So if this offends you in any way, then perhaps this book is not for you. It's okay to just move on. I'd rather you just have a laugh and relax. Life is too short to be stressed about a book. ☺

CHAPTER 1

CHOOSING THE LIFE YOU WANT

- *Are you tired of being sick and tired?*
- *Do you feel trapped by your problem and want to find a way out?*
- *Are you badgered by that critical voice in your mind constantly judging yourself?*
- *Do you want to release suffering and live free and happy as yourself, not who people think you should be?*

If you've read this far, then this book is for you.

I believe that no-one should suffer unnecessarily; I have *learnt* that no-one has to suffer unnecessarily.

I once believed that all suffering was inevitable, that life was one hardship after another. I believed that I was the victim of my circumstances and whatever was going on in my life. Before I learnt the secret to reduce suffering, I had no idea that it didn't have to be this way.

I will always remember the moment when that belief changed, when I realised that I had a choice. I had taken a break from studying psychology. On one very normal day when I walked into my bland corporate job, a thought hit me, 'I just can't do this anymore. I can't walk into this place another day and spend my life not doing what I'm really passionate about'.

I wanted to help people. I needed to help people.

I felt my body physically react to being in that corporate workspace. My stomach churned, my body tightened, my brain resisted. I couldn't keep living incongruently to a deeper call that shouted within me. It was like there was a song in my heart that was determined to be sung. To be expressed. To be alive. I couldn't contain it anymore. I was bursting to be *me*.

Suddenly, I felt in charge of myself, in charge of my circumstances. I would *not* walk in that door one more day and pretend to care about something that I felt didn't make any difference in the world. That one moment changed my life forever.

It wasn't just the set of circumstances that I found myself in. It wasn't just a job that sucked my passion dry. The lightning bolt moment was that I could see that the amount of suffering I endured was optional! The moment this realisation hit me, my mind could not return to "normal". I could see, perhaps for the first time in my life, that regardless of circumstances, I could choose the amount of suffering I endured.

I took charge of my actions. I quit that job and set myself on a new path of empowerment. I decided to make my dreams happen. I returned to pursue my Graduate year at university, I travelled solo on a safari in Africa and I opened myself up to a new relationship. Most importantly I changed my mindset and learnt to stop dwelling on the past.

Before, I would agonise over small moments that upset me, now with this new understanding, I could see and accept those moments for what they were (impressionable and intangible snapshots interpreted in a distorted way within our own minds) and then I knew to either move on or make a change.

THE SECRET TO LIFE

You see, the reason why this moment was so deeply shocking to me was because I had been obsessed with learning about human nature for decades. I sought out endless amounts of education and courses to understand the nature of our minds and behaviours. So this new piece of information, I had discovered quite by accident, at first left me outraged — why hadn't anyone ever told me this before? Why wasn't this in any of my degrees or courses, dammit?

I wanted to yell from the rooftops, "This is the secret to life!"

Ever since that epiphany, I have had a dream that no-one has to suffer unnecessarily. I use the word *suffer* because pain is unavoidable but the amount of suffering is optional. If you are alive and have a heartbeat, there will always be some pain in life, yet we can reduce the amount of unnecessary suffering.

In my role as a psychologist, it is my privilege and honour that people share their lives with me and trust me to guide and support them during difficult times — I do not take this mantle lightly. It is the best job in the world and I am deeply passionate and committed to whatever it takes to help people live their best life. Quitting that corporate job and pursuing psychology like my life depended on it was one of the best decisions I have ever made. It pivoted me to my purpose.

I know this is my purpose and I'm so excited to share these significant lessons with you. I must tell you right off the bat — I have personally benefited from every single lesson I share with you from over the last thirty years. These aren't just theories, they have been through the wringer called my life. I have worked them like an aerobic lesson. I have lived and breathed these strategies. And that's how I know they really work. I am living proof, and so are the hundreds of clients I have shared them with.

Decades of embracing these strategies, alongside my education, clinical practice, training and applied exercises have culminated in being able to finally share this information with you. No bullshit, no jargon. Just *Real Talk, Real Change.*

I want to share the ideas and tools so you can see the power YOU possess to make powerful changes in YOUR life.

It is simple but not easy. However I wouldn't believe in it so much if I hadn't proved it could work in my own life. As they say, "you don't know until you try."

TRAGEDY AND TRANSFORMATION

In 2013, I was pregnant with twin boys. I was super excited and nervous, planning an amazing life together with my then very young daughter and my gorgeous husband in our lovely new home. Then at 23 weeks, after doing everything we could possibly do to keep them, my little boys died three days apart. I gave birth to my sons, stillborn on the 1st of May.

Life was never going to be the same. I was never going to be the same.

However, I had learned many tools and techniques over the years so I knew what to do. With support, I got on with the process of grieving and rebuilding a different life from the one I had ached for and planned so vividly.

This was not the first time I'd had to align myself to a new reality.

I had been married before (then divorced), I'd been a full-time step-mum for five years (then wasn't one), I had returned to study as a mature-age student in the digital world (a few times over the years), I had become an unplanned business owner (who had no idea what she was getting herself into) and life's challenges have continued on. I have had to clear psychological blockages, re-learn and re-adjust each and every time. Reorient myself and pivot to a new life.

You see, very often, the highs and lows of life are intensified by our internal suffering. Of course, pain will be felt but it's the **level of suffering we experience that we have power over.**

You are *not* at the mercy of your circumstances. I know this seems incredible to hear, and for many years I too believed suffering was an inescapable part of life.

But through my study and search for human truth I discovered psychological cycles I was able to break out of and mental techniques that helped me create change. I questioned everything deeply and it began to alter three major things. I began to:

- Recognise the crap my mind was telling me for what it was (which was mostly just unhelpful thoughts).
- Change the things I was doing that weren't working for me.
- Get out of the trap I *thought* I was in and *thought* I had no choice about.

These three simple things were potent life-altering formulas for my new life.

They have been the cornerstone that made me great at reinventing myself and changing my life. I am also great at helping other people to do this too. I work with people to identify what's in the way, deal with it, and then move forward. I do this with and for myself constantly and never-endingly. I am a work in progress and always will be, but aren't we all?! If you're human, trust me, you are a work in progress.

It's just the way life is.

That's what's so exciting. I get to change and reinvent how my life looks, in any way, at any time. I am not perfect (I would never want to be — how boring and unrelatable), but I absolutely do have a stack of tools, knowledge and experience to help people get out of their own way, and go on to create amazing success and happiness in their life.

Yes — you can reinvent yourself too. How cool is that?

THE LIFE YOU WANT

This book is about teaching people how to live the kind of life they want; whether it be big and adventurous or quiet and peaceful, whatever it is it can be their choice.

So, what about you…
What do you want?
What's your choice?
What are your dreams for your life?

This book will show you that you no longer need to suffer unnecessarily. *(I'm going to keep saying that until you believe me!)*

That you have a choice in how you respond when the going gets tough. Yes, it's true — from anxiety, grief, depression, self-doubt and self-esteem issues to relationship and health challenges; my dream is to show you how to rise above these challenges and create a satisfying and fulfilling life for yourself, no matter the circumstances.

So, how do we do this? How can you take your current circumstance and transform it to your wildest dreams?

Hang on to your seat, we're about to take this ride together. Yee-hah!

THE FIRST THING

The first thing you will need to know is how your thoughts and feelings are formed, and the physiology behind them. You will then begin to see how these internal mechanisms are powerful enough to create your experiences and shape your beliefs and behaviours. Ultimately these create the results you see in your life. It's like magic.

So if you're not liking your results, don't worry, they can be changed — you can change them! Truly.

I am going to share with you the tools and techniques that worked for me, the ones that I use in my clinical practice every day. That's why I use them — because they get results. They help people move out of the quagmire of crap they cover themselves in and shine a bright light into the future.

The ideas in this book are based on Cognitive Behavioural Therapy techniques, and though they've been around for a while, I have discovered that they're some of the most effective strategies for people to use for the long-term. Over time I have adapted them to make them super easy to understand and get you moving forward. We don't want complicated techniques do we? We just need what works!

So, whatever battle you're facing, let's take this journey together, so you can finally **Choose the Life You Want!**

Are you ready? Let's do it!

> "Pain is a normal part of living,
> while suffering is optional."
> — Dr Nat

HAVING A VOICE

I'm going to share a little secret with you. When I first thought about writing this book, a little voice crept up and I doubted myself — *who me?* Then I changed that thought and said to myself *'of course I can write a book, I've written hundreds of thousands of words before, maybe more.'*

But the doubts crept back in, talking louder — *'Write about what? What do I possibly have to say that could be worth someone wanting to spend their time reading?'* The negativity continued, *'No really, what do I have to say?'*

And finally the thought that maybe I have nothing to say paralysed me.

Now intellectually, I know that I have a lot to say. I know a lot, I've experienced a lot in life, I've talked to and worked with a lot of people. I've been a non-stop formal learner since I was five years old.

This lifetime of learning includes four university degrees, a doctorate in psychology with a published thesis, around thirty years of attending countless courses in both personal and professional development and reading thousands of books and articles.

If I look back, I intellectually know that I've spent over hundreds of thousands of dollars in pure education and training with the obsessive search of looking for the fastest, most effective tools and strategies for lasting change. And I have many years of experience working with hundreds of clients over thousands of hours.

"There is no greater agony than bearing an untold story inside."[1]
— *Maya Angelou*

Yeah, what would I have to say? Right! Bloody hell. It sounds ridiculous, right? How could I have spent more than fifty years on this planet, have learnt all of that, and still not think I have anything worthwhile to say? Let alone my numerous life experiences and my long and varied career path. It just makes no sense right? Yet, here I was.

FINDING MY VOICE

Now, spending my days talking so much kept resulting in me losing my voice. So I engaged a voice coach to help me learn how to care for my voice and learn how to present and speak the best I could in front of groups. The main message from the voice coach wasn't about my vocal cords. She said, "You're holding back, and it's a psychological issue."

My initial reaction was shock! *What? Are you crazy? How can that be? You have no idea how much work I've done on myself to ensure that my past did not hold me back. I've worked too hard not to be free.* And I was, 'Free; free to be me!' *Wasn't I?*

Plus I speak and write every day, all the time. I've always been a speaker and writer in one way or another. Whether it was as a corporate trainer, an educator, a teacher, or writing reports, assignments, or training materials. I love it, and I've been pretty good at it. It can't possibly be a psychological block, right? I'm a self-aware psychologist and life coach.

But then it dawned on me — none of that work has ever been about me.

It was always about something or someone else. It was never about my own personal opinion or *me* speaking and writing in my own personal style. There was always a structure, a format, a way of writing or speaking that was the formula and needed to be followed. All of my speaking and writing was objective, scientific, about a topic or issue. It was not about having a personal opinion or written or spoken in my own unique way.

I had rarely been asked to give my own opinion and thoughts and ideas about things. In fact, when I think about it, if I ever was asked, and I barely remember this happening, my memory of it is that I couldn't speak — I had nothing to say!

Very different than if I was asked for the answer to a factual question, or to speak on a given topic, or to research a subject. Even in university, answers were always based on other people's research and facts, and reports were formulaic. Never was it about me in the unique way I could express myself or my own personal thoughts about things.

'Don't speak or write unless you have the facts, done in a specific way, on a specific topic — we *don't* want just your opinion.' So I took that on board. Self-expression and creativity squashed, right there. Who cares what I think or want? Who cares what I have to say or what I've learnt? Even though deep down I know that I have so much to share that could possibly help people.

But you know what? I don't think I'm alone. I think there are many people like me, men and women who unconsciously hold back, thinking that they don't have much to say, written or spoken, and certainly nothing worthwhile anyway.

And even though we know it is not true intellectually; emotionally — it's what we do. You know the inner patterns — don't offend anyone, don't say the wrong thing, don't look stupid, don't have a go. *Don't, don't, don't, don't. Blah, blah, blah.*

Well here's an ambitious idea…what about not giving a shit about what others think or say? Yep. You heard me right. How about you try that on for size!

This is your psychologist and life coach saying, "Let's not hold back, don't worry if you get it wrong, don't die wondering if you were the one who could have made a difference in the world by saying what there is to be said."

This book is about reclaiming YOU! About finding you and your beautiful voice once and for all. About learning how to take your power back and not give a flying f#ck what other people think or say about you. I've got your back. You have a voice with me. Right here.

And guess what?

I'm risking it too. This is my first book and I want to give you my unique voice; as vulnerable and scary as it feels for me sometimes — I don't want to hold back anymore either. I want to stand up and be counted, and I want you to do the same.

What is it that YOU have to say?
What are you holding back on?
What kind of difference could you make in the world if you did speak out?
How would it feel to live wildly alive as YOU?

I bet it would feel pretty damn good! And it should. I bet you're awesome.

In my quest to find my own voice, I came to a deeper knowing. I realised that my desire to help others have great lives is far stronger than my desire for me to stay small and not say anything. I'm willing to risk it and have a go, to step out, to be free to express myself and say what there is to say, in the hope that this helps you too. So, here goes…

Let's hold hands and do this together.

*"Take a chance, speak up,
you're totally worth it!"*

— Dr Nat

CHAPTER 2

YOU'RE NOT ALONE — I PROMISE!

I'm going to bet that you've had some really shit things happen in your life. The fact that you're reading this book indicates that you probably have. I know those shitty times must have been hard; really hard. I'm really sorry that you've experienced pain and grief in your life. It sucks. It's tough and often unfair.

It can be incredibly painful when you first realise that life can be both tough and unfair. It's like a burning reality slap in the face — I know because I've had my fair share too.

As a psychologist and life coach, I've met a lot of people who've experienced some really terrible and heartbreaking circumstances, and the harsh thing about life is that no-one is immune to these things. No one can avoid life's challenges. The fact is: if you live long enough, life will inevitably deal you some ridiculously challenging situations.

I know this sounds like really bad news, depressing even, but there is something very important to realise about this fact, and that is; **you are *not* alone.** Every human being at some stage faces some sort of life challenge or setback. You are not alone, nor singled out.

Now, I know it may seem like you're the only one experiencing this pain because it feels so intimate and personal — but let me assure you, you most definitely are not. Just because you haven't heard anyone else talk about the crap they're dealing with doesn't mean they're not going through it. People can hide so much pain behind a smile.

You see, it's our innate survival instinct to not want to let others know that we are not okay. This is because back in caveman days, the so-called 'weakest' person got ousted or left behind. That person was likely to be eaten by a sabre tooth tiger.

In our evolutionary story, it was good to be strong for survival. And although this instinct has been about needing physical strength for survival, in our modern world we have interpreted this to mean to be strong in general — including emotional and mental strength. And so, we keep that stiff upper lip, we maintain a facade of being "strong" and therefore, okay, even if we don't feel it.

But we must evolve from this outdated way of perceiving strength as it's really just a mask, a cover-up of the truth. I'd like to say that's it outdated and old-fashioned. True strength is so much more than physical.

THE UPS AND DOWNS OF LIFE

I often tell my clients to imagine life like a hospital monitor, you know the ones you see in the movies going *beep, beep, beep*. The machine keeps time with your heartbeat, and the line of the graph goes up and down along with your vital signs.

LIFE IS KIND OF LIKE THIS

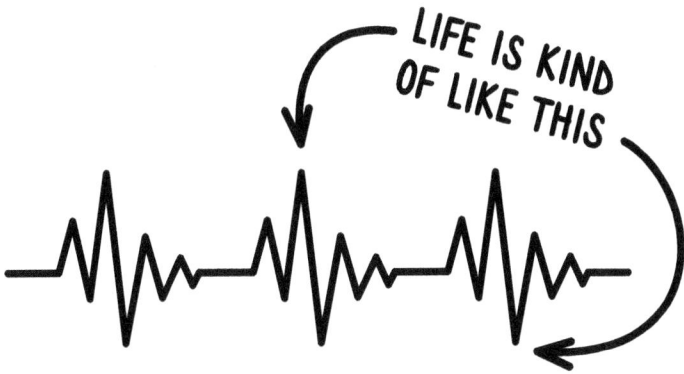

The graph on the machine keeps going up and down like a series of endless hills and while our heart is beating — then we are alive. So, the way I see it, as long as we're alive, life will go up (yay!) ...and down (boo!), just like this machine. As long as this graph continues going up *and* down, it is a GOOD thing because it means that we're alive (yay!).

There is only really a problem: when the graph flatlines! This is not good. However, some people think that it's a good place to be and they want to stay there — in a very flat life, without any turmoil or movement. But I'm convinced this is worse. Why? Because flatlining through your life means you aren't truly living and you're closer to being dead than alive. That's not real living in my opinion. It may be existing but it's not living fully.

It is actually when we have those peaks and troughs that we know that we're truly alive and living. These moments are where true growth happens, where all the learning, the understanding, the appreciation takes place. Now, don't get me wrong, I know it can be very painful and unwanted at times, but it's the biggest indicator that we are actually alive *and living*.

> "Because being alive and living aren't
> exactly the same thing."
> — Dr Nat

Let me tell you why. Now, you can be alive and flatlining — which means that you're not involved in life and just observing from the sidelines. Alive but not engaged in life. Alive but just existing. Alive but just observing life pass you by. A bystander.

Or you can be alive and two-feet-in. Alive and feeling the peaks and troughs. Alive and engaged as an active member of the planet. Alive and dancing in the high and lows of real living.

Now here's the thing every human needs to know — as long as you're alive and living, shit will happen to you! Fullstop!

And it will happen to everyone else too! You can't escape the clutches of life's ups and downs, because that's the nature of life. Trees grow, flowers bloom, bees buzz, dogs bark…and well life goes up and down. That's its very nature.

But it's from these depths that we can then truly appreciate the peaks — the good fortune, the health and happiness, the big celebrations. We can truly taste what it's like to live. Otherwise we have nothing to compare it to and it would all just blend together in one boring and uneventful existence.

Now, I know what you may be thinking. That a flat, boring uneventful experience would be a cakewalk instead of the pain and grief you may be currently experiencing. That a boring grey existence would be a welcome relief from the emotional rollercoaster you're on right now.

It's normal to want the pain to stop. In fact, it's a great motivation to have because it means that you want better in your life, that you are willing to try new things in order to change your state.

Let me ask you this: have you ever been really sick at some point in your life? Then one day, almost like a miracle, you woke up feeling better and said — *'wow, I really feel a whole lot better, I didn't realise how sick I was.'*

You truly appreciate feeling better!

Now, for some reason, humans seem to learn through experience more than theory. So, you have to *experience* the difference from one state to another. In other words, the ecstasy, the joy is sweeter because of the mundane or challenging moments.

Now, don't get me wrong. I can still hear you shouting, "I don't care! I don't want any pain even if it helps me experience the joy more."

And guess what, you're right. But as you'll hear me say throughout this book, life's nature is like that machine — it will *always* go up and down whether you want it to or not. And what I suggest to my clients is — get good with that harsh fact first. Because just like your height or eye colour — it's a fact you can't change.

LOSING YOUR SH*T

Now, maybe that thought of not being able to change life's up and downs makes you want to lose your shit. Fair enough. It's normal for shit to happen in all of our lives, I can also tell you that it's okay to lose your shit sometimes. You wouldn't be human if you didn't and we all do it, including me!

No matter how amazing we are, no matter how smart, well-educated, successful, spiritual or enlightened we are, we can still stumble and fall under the sheer weight of living.

Losing your shit sometimes isn't a shameful thing, it's a human thing. Because remember, we are all human beings bumbling along doing the best we can with what we have and what we know. And because we are experiencing all the highs and lows of life in their raw and unpredictable glory — and doing it all without a manual or guide map — sometimes we'll lose our shit.

Sometimes we'll swear like a trooper and growl like a wild animal. But once we calm down, we often realise how human we are, and that's okay. How the stress or pressure of uncertainty can make anyone feel a little extra edgy and scared. It also helps us better understand and empathise with our fellow human beings.

This type of empathy makes us better humans and allows us to experience a greater depth of love and connection — and personally, I wouldn't trade that for anything.

We *all* go through hardship, directly or indirectly at some point throughout our lives. No one is immune. There is no vaccination for this.

REAL TALK FOR REAL CHANGE

- We all have pain, the amount of suffering is optional.
- It's normal to have ups and downs in life — it's mandatory for a life well-lived.
- The hard times in life remind us and help us to appreciate the good things in life.
- We can all lose our shit — no matter how smart or phenomenal we are — it's called being human!

CHAPTER 3

WHEN YOUR BUCKET IS FULL

Most people who come to see me as a psychologist are in the midst of some kind of crisis or have concerns about what's going on for them. Mostly there are two questions they initially have. *'What's wrong with me?'* and, *'Am I normal?'* Part of my job is to help them identify the real problem, discuss the likely explanation as to why they are feeling turmoil or acting in a negative way, and then work together with that person to learn some strategies or tools to overcome that issue.

As humans we naturally want to make sense of what's happening and why we feel the way we do. Our brains really like 'knowing' (certainty) and they really don't like 'not knowing' (uncertainty). The inner drive to know *why* and to have an explanation is a biological survival mechanism; we've relied on our knowledge of the world around us to survive for millennia, so it's quite a powerful driver behind our decisions and actions.

THE STRESS RESPONSE THAT LIES INSIDE YOU

When I see a client for the first time, I often begin with an explanation about the human stress response. This response stems from the ancient biology of our caveman days.

Here's what I share with them.

In our caveman days we had to depend on our physiological system to keep us alert and away from danger. So back then for example, sabre-toothed tigers created real life-threatening stress! Imagine; you'd be sitting in your cave feeling nice and safe and when it came time to venture out for food (no Uber Eats back then!) you needed to be physically and mentally on guard for any dangers as you scouted around. This vigilance was about sensing mortal danger that was likely to jump out and kill you! Pretty heavy, right? But the mechanism was there to protect you.

So if you ever did face a sabre-toothed tiger, this stress trigger would register in your brain as a threat (a stressor) and your body would kick in an urgent physiological response that enabled you to either 'fight' the threat, or run the hell away (that is, take 'flight'). You may have heard of this and know it as our 'fight or flight' response.

There is also another less known response which is the 'freeze' response, which can occur when you are absolutely paralysed by fear. It's akin to a 'playing dead' response for when we feel completely trapped, or hopeless about the situation (the stressor) and it feels like we have no other option.

More specifically this fight-flight-freeze response is set off by a quick evaluation or perception that the 'stress' we have come up against is a danger to our well-being. In caveman days, this was about a physical threat or danger, so our clever mind and body developed a survival mechanism to instinctively decide in an instant whether to stay and fight or run the hell away. Pretty clever, hey?

Human brains naturally look for the physical reasoning behind their feelings and actions and we also like hearing an immediate and logical explanation for what's going on. Makes sense when you remember that ancient part of our brain helped us do this in times of crisis.

This survival mechanism is triggered by the 'perception' that something is dangerous. If I suddenly saw a sabre-toothed tiger and last week I had seen my neighbour Joe eaten by one of them (yes, Joe lives in the cave next door) then I'd know that my situation was dire! Once we perceive something as dangerous, our sympathetic nervous system kicks into immediate action.

So, how does it do this?

Well, it gets us going by sending signals from our brain to release chemicals such as adrenaline and cortisol. These chemicals increase our heart rate to quickly pump blood to areas such as arm and leg muscles for extra oxygen and nutrients for running and fighting. This means some areas of our body, such as our digestive system and much of our brain, then receives less blood flow than normal. These areas are deemed less important in the moment of survival, while arms and legs are very important for running and fighting.

This is why when we are stressed we sometimes feel nauseous and lose our appetite, because there's less blood flow in the stomach. Importantly, when we experience a decrease in blood flow to some areas of the brain, such as the prefrontal cortex, it's because it's deemed unnecessary for us to be doing high-level thinking at this time.

The only options your brain wants you to be considering are — run or fight — run or fight! That's it! That's it's entire agenda.

So, when we are under stress, our psyche downshifts into the older and more primitive part of our brain — the survival part; the amygdala. Subsequently, we may find it more difficult to concentrate, make decisions, be creative or solve problems. You probably know this feeling. We all have experienced it at some time.

More blood gets pumped into important areas for survival and less pumped to those places that aren't needed right then. Energy or sugars also get released from our stores during this response. These increase and circulate in the bloodstream to assist with fast energy available for running and fighting. Hence, for those of us with diabetes and blood sugar issues, it is likely to make more sense as to why and how stress can cause issues with maintaining consistent blood sugar levels.

In addition, during this response our muscles become tense to increase our strength and speed for running and fighting. All of this is a sympathetic nervous system response — all very important things when you are trying to survive a physical threat like a sabre-toothed tiger.

Physical threat responses need to be automatic, fast and immediate to get us out of danger! After we are out of danger, we take a rest and calm down, perhaps sitting around the fire celebrating our escape and hopefully eating a nice meal of sabre-toothed tiger steak! Ahhhh we wind down. No reality TV back then.

While this response was super amazing for the past and still is when we are in physical danger, it is not so helpful when there is a non-physical threat. This fight or flight response was designed to be a *once-every-now-and-then* reaction, releasing adrenaline for the occasional physical threat. Great for back then when they didn't have many non-physical threats or worries. Not so great for now.

Our threats and worries look very different today, don't they?

What if I fail my exam? How will I know if she likes me? What if I miss my deadline? What if I make an idiot of myself in front of them? How will I pay all these bills? What if I lose my job or get sick?

Those old caveman physical threats were not the ongoing, never-ending, cramming our minds from dawn 'til dusk non-physical threats (or thoughts) that we have today. Those ancient threats were short, finite and physical — perfect for the stress response we had developed over time — clever humans! However, it's a terrible response for today's non-physical threats and worries.

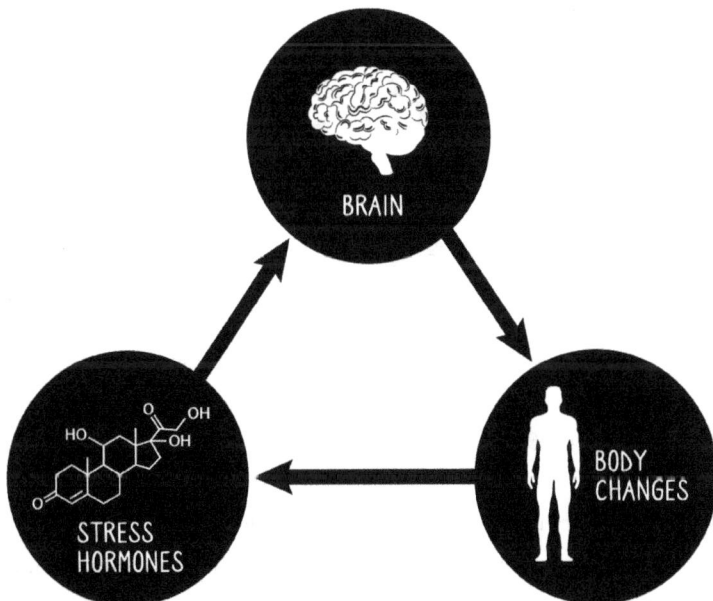

STEPS TO FREEDOM
YOU AND YOUR STRESS

Step 1. Understanding that we naturally have this inbuilt mechanism to know WHY we feel the way we do, is the first step to our freedom. Why? Because it gives us a practical understanding of our behaviour and often some initial relief that we're absolutely *normal*. That it's normal to try and 'get our head around' things. That there's nothing abnormal about feeling some turmoil during uncertainty.

So, if you are grappling to make sense of your situation, or perhaps feel a little anxious about the unpredictable dilemma you find yourself in — your primitive brain is wired to try and understand it. And when this happens, it's often quite normal to ask: What's happening to me? What's wrong with me? Am I normal?

It's just the brains patterning and attempts to try and understand the situation. It's not abnormal, okay? In fact, it's chronically normal.

You're wired this way.

So, the first step to freedom is: **Know That What You're Experiencing is Normal.**

Step 2. When I help people identify what is specifically causing the problem (which may not always be the most obvious source), I help people recognise that there is a logical explanation as to why they are feeling or acting the way that they are, and that there's something that can be done about it. It helps to know there is a solution, even if we don't have it just yet.

Let me explain. Commonly many people that come to see me are everyday people who are experiencing some form of stress, either multiple stresses or perhaps one form of stress has triggered another. They come in for help because they don't know how to manage their situation.

For example, one of my clients — let's call her Maggie, had a boss who was stressing her out. Maggie began to feel anxious and depressed and didn't know how to deal with her boss. In order to cope with her unwanted emotions she began to drink a little more alcohol than usual every night and soon began having sleeping troubles. She woke up anxious and unable to face a day at work to deal with her boss. Her partner became upset by her behaviour and they started to fight more than ever. The cycle becomes a vicious one. What began as one problem quickly avalanched into several. See how the problem became more? It can make someone feel caught in a negative spiral.

So, in situations like these, it helps to identify the actual source of the problem. For example, in Maggie's case, the underlying issue was that Maggie had been bullied as a child, so when anything remotely felt like or reminded her of this time, she freaked out and became extremely stressed and anxious.

Addressing the cause of the problem will help to eliminate it, rather than just managing the symptoms. If we break the pattern of her distress from being bullied then it is likely that she will be better able to manage present and future stressors.

Sometimes it can be helpful to get a professional to assist you in this area.

So the second step to freedom is: **Identify the Real Problem.**

But of course, Maggie isn't alone. Everyone to some degree is dealing with "stuff".

It could be losing a job, the death of a loved-one, battling health problems, relationship breakdowns, financial hardships. All of these things can create significant stress and turmoil in our lives. Sometimes we have the energy, resources, tools and support around us to help us move forward in these trials and sometimes we don't.

Chronic stress is like running away from hundreds of sabre-tooth tigers every day, it's exhausting and you end up depleted.

One day we're going along doing okay, and then the next — we're not. Some people have a number of stressors that start to pile up and it just becomes too much, or sometimes it is the one stressor over a long period of time that just wears us and our resources down and we need extra help.

Some people just need someone to bounce ideas off. Someone who is neutral, non-judgmental, objective, who has their best interests at heart and won't (or shouldn't) talk about their own crap or experiences or tell them what they *should* be doing.

It could be that someone just needs to talk to a person who has the training and capacity to fully listen so they don't have to worry about the impact of what they're saying on the listener's welfare or what they will do with that information, knowing it is confidential.

Everyone is unique in what they require to get through their crisis or change.

But there's something we all have in common and that is...an emotion bucket.

THE EMOTION BUCKET

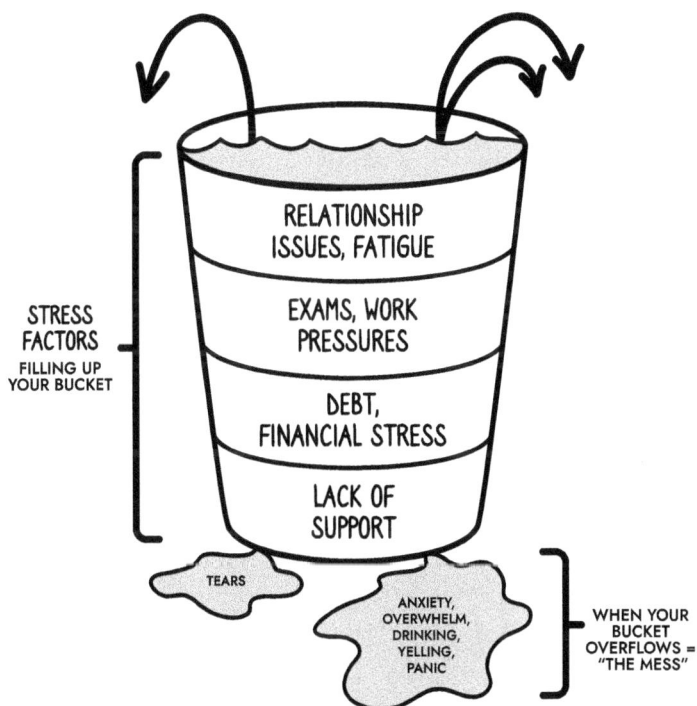

Regardless of the situation, we each have an Emotion Bucket (I do love a good visual!).

Okay, you may not actually see it like your nose or arms, but believe me, you have it. You can't see your spleen but you have one, right?

Now, this Emotion Bucket can cope with a lot when shit happens and it starts to fill up with stress and emotions. Sometimes we do okay with managing our bucket and sometimes we don't do so well. If we don't manage our Emotion Bucket in a healthy way, it will start to overflow at some point and crap will spill out all over the place.

THE EMOTION BUCKET

STRESS FACTORS
FILLING UP YOUR BUCKET

RELATIONSHIP ISSUES, FATIGUE

EXAMS, WORK PRESSURES

DEBT, FINANCIAL STRESS

LACK OF SUPPORT

TEARS

ANXIETY, OVERWHELM, DRINKING, YELLING, PANIC

WHEN YOUR BUCKET OVERFLOWS = "THE MESS"

This is when we start to see some mess around — teariness, forgetfulness, increased alcohol use, yelling at the kids, a general feeling of not coping, being overwhelmed.

This is a sign — **it's time to empty your Emotion Bucket!**

It's important to find ways of doing that regularly, before it fills up and overflows with crap again.

Our job is to identify firstly what stressors fill up your bucket as it's different for everyone. Then how you can most effectively and efficiently empty it. Again, there are different ways to do this for everyone. It's good to figure out how to maintain it at a manageable level so it doesn't keep filling up and overflowing completely. And yes — again it's different for everyone so it takes some time to work through those solutions.

WHAT'S IN YOUR EMOTION BUCKET?

List all the things that are contributing to filling up your stress and emotion bucket. For example, being over-committed, constantly working long days, kids having busy schedules, over-eating, perfectionism, excessive worry, over-responsibility. Write them all down.

Step 3. The third step to freedom is: find ways to **Change, Better Manage, or Empty Some Things in Your Bucket**.

HOW TO STOP YOUR EMOTION BUCKET FROM BUILDING UP TOO HIGH, BECOMING UNMANAGEABLE, AND OVERFLOWING

- **Identify things you can change and things you can't.** Apply this strategy where it best works for you in a particular situation — for example, mandatory home schooling is something I can't change but yelling at the kids is something that I can change — so I can work on not yelling (staying calm) because yelling just makes it worse, then I feel bad and they feel bad. And nobody needs that in their bucket.

- **Learn coping skills.** Ask yourself: What gets me through the things that I cannot change or cannot change right now? — e.g. going for a run, talking or venting to a friend, having a laugh, painting, having a bath. Write a list and keep it nearby, that way you always have something that you could do at hand.

- **Re-frame issues.** See things from a different perspective — it could be from someone else's perspective (i.e. stand in their shoes, look at it from an outside persepective) or it could be using other ways to describe this issue — for example, I am a burden to others versus I just need more compassion to care for myself. Or ask yourself: what would I say to my best friend about this? Then say that to yourself instead.

- **Discuss issues with a trusted friend.** Find someone who can just listen to you without interrupting and telling their own story — you can actually ask people to do this! And you can ask for their help or their opinion if you want that too.

- **Re-prioritise issues.** How important is this thing in the scheme of things right now? Do I need to address this right now? Can this issue be put to the bottom of the list? Or be delayed until next month? (This is equally good for overwhelm too). Say to yourself something like "I'm deciding not to decide right now. I will revisit this in an hour (or maybe a day, a week, next month)." Then schedule it in for that time, and forget about it until then.

- **Change focus.** For example, focus on the growth you're getting right now, versus the stress. When I was grieving for my boys, rather than constantly focusing on the grief, I would say to myself — "This is just for now, it's not forever, one day this pain will subside and it will help me to help someone else." I would then refocus my attention on something else. I might do something that either felt like it was an achievement (no matter how small) or something that made me feel joy or happiness. I did this over and over, many times, until I didn't need to anymore.

- **Ask better questions of yourself.** Instead of asking "Why did this happen to me?" perhaps you could ask, "How can I do it differently next time?" "What can I learn from this experience that is positive and helpful for me and for my future?" There are hundreds of great questions we can ask ourselves (or someone else) that will lead us down a way better pathway than the shitty questions we often ask ourselves like, "Why me?". These questions lead nowhere and give you nothing but more suffering.

- **6 Steps to Use Problem Solving Frames**
  When we have some control in an issue, using a problem solving approach can be useful. Often the most important step

is clearly defining the actual problem. Be very specific about what the actual issue is so that you get a solution that solves the actual problem. Again, this can be tricky and sometimes getting a professional to help you define what the real problem is can be helpful. Here are the problem-solving steps:

1. Define the problem
2. Gather information
3. Generate and brainstorm possible solutions
4. Evaluate the ideas and then choose one
5. Implement the idea
6. Evaluate the results

If the result is not what you wanted or is not working then you can go back and either select a different solution, generate more possible solutions, or start again and redefine the problem. You can find lots more information on the internet about problem solving frames and each of these steps.

- **Check-in with Self.** Ask yourself, "How am I feeling right now? What do I need right now?" Listen to what your mind comes back with and implement what is most practical and appropriate (I say this because sometimes my brain says I need a holiday for six months in the Bahamas and this is not practical or appropriate — but I get the idea that I need a break and will make this happen in line with my responsibilities and needs).

- **Feel good activities.** Engage in activities just for you, things that make you feel good or happy, give you some kind of pleasure — do it regularly — something small each day, something medium each week, something bigger each month. It's your job!

- **Achievement activities.** Do things (small things or big things broken down into small chunks) that make you feel that you have achieved something each day, then pat yourself on the back for doing it (literally!). And then say to yourself (when no-one is watching of course!) "Good job!" The more you do that, the better you'll feel, and the more you'll want to do it, and the better you'll feel, and...well, I'm sure you get the picture.

> *"We are all just human beings, bumbling along doing the best we can. When we know better, we do better."*
> *— Dr Nat*

- **Get resourceful.** Getting resourceful is especially good for those who do it all themselves, and feel that they must do everything on their to-do list. Get clear about:
  - » What you're good at
  - » What you want to do or need to do
  - » What someone else could do or help you with
  - » What could be deleted or doesn't need to be done anymore — what's urgent or important, what can wait, who could you swap services with, is there another way?

- **Talk to a Professional.** Let someone help you, someone who can listen and guide you in the right direction. Please remember, all therapists and coaches and clinicians are different and have different approaches and styles. You may not "click" with the first person, or even the second or third. It's like trying to find a great hairdresser or GP. Don't give up until you get someone who you believe can meet your needs.

THE CALM FACTOR THAT LIES WITH YOU (YES, YOU HAVE ONE!)

So now you know how your inbuilt stress system responds and you know how to empty your emotion bucket. Now, it's time to know how to trigger your feel-good mojo.

FiGHt oR FLiGHt   ReLaxeD to tHe Max

SYMPATHETIC   PARASYMPATHETIC

So, you have a **sympathetic nervous system** and a **parasympathetic nervous system**.

The fight or flight response triggers your sympathetic nervous system to rapidly prepare the body for fighting, fleeing or freezing. The heart races, the muscles pump, and the body gets primed for ready, fast action. On the other hand, the parasympathetic nervous system is the system that restores the body to a calm and composed state, it slows the heart rate. It is sometimes called the rest and digest system. It stays switched off while the sympathetic system is on, and vice versa, when the parasympathetic nervous system is on, the sympathetic system is switched off.

When we don't need to fight or flee our sympathetic system response becomes very unhelpful for us, you could say it does the opposite of what we need at that particular time. For example, when we have a problem to solve, we need to be super chilled and to be in a parasympathetic nervous system response, which enables lots of blood flow to the brain. This increases oxygen and nutrients, so we can think clearly and use the most developed part of our brain, the part that thinks logically, makes decisions, concentrates and problem-solves; this part of the brain is known as our prefrontal cortex.

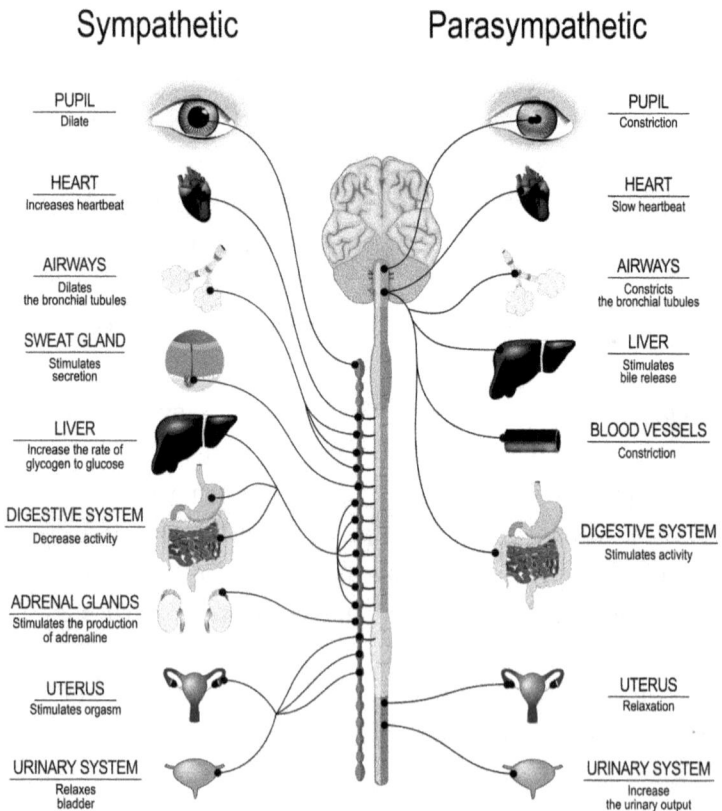

Sympathetic   Parasympathetic

PUPIL	PUPIL
Dilate	Constriction

HEART	HEART
Increases heartbeat	Slow heartbeat

AIRWAYS	AIRWAYS
Dilates the bronchial tubules	Constricts the bronchial tubules

SWEAT GLAND	LIVER
Stimulates secretion	Stimulates bile release

LIVER	BLOOD VESSELS
Increase the rate of glycogen to glucose	Constriction

DIGESTIVE SYSTEM	DIGESTIVE SYSTEM
Decrease activity	Stimulates activity

ADRENAL GLANDS	
Stimulates the production of adrenaline	

UTERUS	UTERUS
Stimulates orgasm	Relaxation

URINARY SYSTEM	URINARY SYSTEM
Relaxes bladder	Increase the urinary output

For us to be most productive and creative in our problem solving, we need our sympathetic nervous system to 'shut the hell up', and we need our parasympathetic nervous system (our relaxation system) to be switched on. This gives us the best chance to work out what we need to do about our problem.

So how can we get the Sympathetic nervous system to shut the hell up? What would make this superhero pipe down?

Well, firstly you need to do things that you find calming and relaxing, especially when you are stressed. It also explains why it sometimes feels like the hardest thing in the world to do. Because you are all amped up on, 'go, go, go!' chemicals (fight-flight) but what you really need to do is, 'chill, chill, chill!' Understanding this contradiction can be helpful so you don't feel like you're going crazy. It also helps you persist with the relaxation stuff because it's so important from a biological perspective. Even if you feel like you're faking it a little, keep going, it's a great start.

HOW TO TAKE THE EDGE OFF

Sometimes I suggest that people go for a quick run or do some strong exercise to help burn off the chemicals such as adrenaline and cortisol, and also to restore more balanced levels of oxygen and carbon dioxide. Then it's good to engage in some kind of relaxation and calming activity. Perhaps a hot bath or shower, a gentle walk in nature, a massage, calming music, maybe even some painting or colouring. It might be doing more focused activities such as meditation, mindfulness, diaphragmatic breathing techniques or body scanning. Choose whatever it is for you that helps you to feel calm, safe and okay.

If it's been a really stress-inducing week, one of the things that I like to do is to go to the movies by myself. I take a hot chocolate, sit in those big recliner seats up the back of the theatre and I completely switch off for a couple of hours. A massage is helpful too and I often use some diaphragmatic breathing techniques. This is because when we are stressed we often hold our breath or shallow breathe.

Doing some long breaths out (like in the 4-7-8 technique) can be awesome. We want to bring our body down and into a state of calm so that we can think straight and develop ways to better manage the stressor. In a calm and relaxed state we can then use our logical, rational and problem solving part of our brain (the prefrontal cortex) to be able to work out how to address the stress.

CHILLAX TO THE MAX — THE 4-7-8 TECHNIQUE

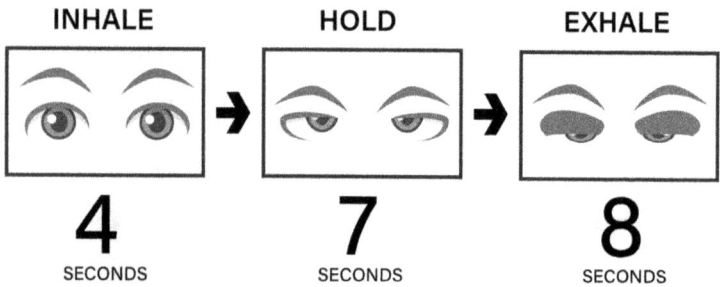

INHALE	HOLD	EXHALE
4 SECONDS	7 SECONDS	8 SECONDS

Step 4. Make Chill Time an Absolute Must!

This is why our first responders are trained to stay very calm when there is a major stressor (think blazing house fires, car accidents, heart attacks). The calmer they stay, the better they can think to process and prioritise what they need to do to overcome the problem. Imagine a fireman running around in circles, all stressed out and yelling crazily at everyone (like a comedy skit!). It just wouldn't work. They have been trained to stay very calm, they practise this and have learnt to calmly and rationally problem-solve issues. Problem-solving cannot be done in a fight and flight mode.

And here's the thing — if these emergency workers can do it when they really should be running away screaming (a physical danger is present and therefore fight and flight should be activated), then we can train ourselves how to do it when we are stressed out about exams or work or anything! Yes it takes effort and can be tricky, but it is absolutely possible with time, effort and persistence.

Practising and implementing calming techniques consistently and frequently, allows us to keep our stress levels lower over time. Rather than having stress build up over the day and ending up at a 9 out of 10 on the stress scale; instead it's better to do short frequent calming exercises throughout the day to keep stress levels lower so we don't keep peaking and ending up in fight and flight mode.

I'd rather that people take 2-3 minutes to do some breathing or a quick mindfulness exercise, or a 5-minute walk a few times per day, than be manic by the end of the day and have to take a lot longer to bring their body down and manageable again.

So, the ultimate thing to do is relaxation and calming techniques as often and as much as possible, shorter and more frequent is always the preferred over one long session.

Being more often in this state of calm, helps us to be **conscious** and **connected**. We become more connected to our bodies and minds and more conscious of the control we have over them. It keeps us aware of how we feel and what we need, but also keeps stress levels lower overall. It is also a skill to be learned so the more frequently we practise, the easier it gets.

When our mind starts to realise that we are okay and safe and not about to be eaten by a sabre-toothed tiger, then it will allow the body to relax more. Yay!

CHRONIC STRESS VERSUS USUAL STRESS

Sometimes though, we have been feeling overwhelmed and stressed for a long period of time. Or there has been an accumulation of many stressors over a short period of time. Both can result in a substantial amount of stress that can impact the mental, physical and emotional wellbeing of a person in a very unhelpful way. Often I will talk with people about this and discuss how confident they may be feeling to implement more helpful strategies, or to change the way they are doing things, or to be able to take some time out, or change their thinking patterns.

Depending upon the outcome of this evaluation, we may discuss the possibility of seeing a qualified physician or practitioner to discuss using some natural or pharmaceutical medication to help them reduce symptoms, so that they are then better able to implement some of the more psychological strategies.

Sometimes doing this helps in certain situations, but it is often suggested that when undertaking pharmaceutical treatment that psychological work should be done alongside this. This is because medication very often only addresses the symptoms and not the causes. Without addressing the cause, we know that the situation is not likely to change over time. Like most things, getting to the cause of something allows us to better understand it and then do something about it for the long term.

Remember of course, that there will always be normal everyday things that we can expect to feel big emotions about — sadness when someone dies, anger when we experience being wronged, a trauma response when something happens that threatens our life or the life of someone close to us. These feelings are normal and important and it is okay and expected that we have these. With support, self-care and acknowledgement, we can expect that over time these feelings will resolve in some ways and that we can return to our usual functioning.

There is only an issue if these feelings *do not* resolve over a period of time. If these feelings prevent the person from moving forward and living a functional and satisfying life. So if you've had some big shit happen, suddenly or over a long period of time, then we may expect that you will feel shit or not operate quite like you were prior to it happening. Remember it's a beep on our life's monitor and it's okay and *normal* — at least for a period of time, let's not forget that!

Similarly we shouldn't forget that there are also some every day, normal events that can cause us to feel an increase in tension and stress; such as having an exam, learning how to drive or going on a first date. We can expect some increased stress in these situations. It's all okay and normal. I know that sometimes people who have had a lot of stress and anxiety in the past may get concerned when they start to experience these feelings again, but always remember there is also a 'normal' level or 'usual' time when our stress may increase for a short period of time. In fact it can be a good thing at times, and help us to become motivated to get into action. Using the tools and techniques can certainly help better manage this stress, but it is normal and okay to feel some of it sometimes.

Also, I'm a big advocate for getting help (did you guess that?). If you don't know what is usual versus what is chronic or unhelpful for you — seek some help. Talk with someone who sees people every day to help establish what is needed and how you can begin to move forward in your life.

The fifth step to freedom is: **Seek professional help if you need it.**

FIVE STEPS TO STRESS FREEDOM
1. Know That What You're Experiencing is Normal
2. Identify the Real Problem
3. Empty Your Emotion Bucket
4. Make Chill Time a Must
5. Get Professional Help If You Need It

REAL TALK FOR REAL CHANGE

- Experiencing stressful feelings is normal — don't freak out — there is nothing wrong with you. You are wired with a "stress button".
- Ongoing stress or a lot of stressful things in a short period of time can take a toll — don't be afraid of getting some support or resources.
- Know how to empty your bucket when you need to.
- Learn how to breathe yourself to calm. (It is scientifically verified to work).
- Although it feels difficult, it is possible to master calming yourself — it's a skill to be learnt. Chill time is essential to engage your parasympathethic system.

CHAPTER 4

THINK — FEEL — DO

For so many years it was a mystery to me why my feelings and reactions to situations didn't seem the same as those I witnessed in other people. Or at times, I would feel and react differently in the same situation. What the hell was that all about? It was weird that we are all human, experiencing the same event or situation, but having very different reactions. How could that be? Was there something wrong with me or maybe something wrong with them?

For example, one time (a long time ago now) I was at a live training event, learning about a "new" therapy called 'ACT' (Acceptance and Commitment Therapy) with Dr Russ Harris. At this training I was in the company of some child and adolescent clinicians, and some of their managers. We were all receiving the very same training course at the same event, but boy-oh-boy, we were having some very different reactions. My thoughts were, "*Oh wow, this is great stuff, it will be fantastic to try out with some of my clients. It really demonstrates the concept of mindfulness well."* I was participating fully in the exercises and really excited. That was me and my experience.

The managers were sitting back watching, not participating, and said that the training was very good, and could be further investigated into how it could be applied at the clinic.

The child and adolescent clinicians were reacting very differently again. They were angry and upset and were saying (out loud to Russ) that the training was a joke and how could this even start to compare to the work that they did already. They refused to do the exercises and basically boycotted the training. I was mortified and I could not understand their reactions at all. *What was wrong with them? Or what was wrong with me — was I missing something?* As it turns out there was nothing wrong with any of us.

WHY WE BEHAVE SO DIFFERENTLY — MYSTERY SOLVED!

Gradually in my quest to understand human nature and how our fascinating mind works, I discovered some gold nuggets of knowledge. It felt like discovering the key to the universe — to understanding everything! Well, perhaps a slight exaggeration but it was a major turning point. Learning why we behave the way we do helped me to personally shift and change my own reactions. This was beyond cool, as though I had uncovered a very big secret. I walked around in astonishment asking myself, *"Why hasn't anyone ever told me these things before?"* I now "get it". I know why people react so differently in different sets of circumstances. Eureka! I had struck gold.

So, I'm going to give you my simplest explanation of the model that astounded me. The model to which so many of my clients respond, "Ah, of course, no wonder; that makes sense to me now." This by no means covers all of the factors that can impact on our experience, and it's not a one-way model. I'm just using the simplest and most direct way to explain this so that you get the benefit of understanding it as well as the confidence to make changes for yourself. I'm guessing that you prefer to take the short fast route rather than me bore you with complexities, right?

My motto has always been, **'do what works'** — so this is my what-actually-works-in-real-life explanation. This will provide enough insight so that you absorb it, understand it and get on with using the parts that work for you.

In the past, I assumed it was the incident itself that caused me to feel certain emotions. I used to say, *"If only that hadn't happened, then I wouldn't feel this way."* Do you know this feeling? I bet you do. We all do it at some point.

If only he loved me, I'd feel okay.

If only she earned more money, we'd be happier.

If only that didn't happen, I'd be healthy.

When I figured out that it wasn't the actual event that caused my emotions — my life changed.

Because if it was the actual event that changed my emotions, then I was at the mercy of whatever external (or internal) events happened. And this was how I once thought it was. To be honest it was a pretty shitty way to live; having no say in what happened to me or in the feelings and reactions that arose from these situations.

But I started to wonder, if it was the actual event that caused us to feel a certain way, then why do we all have such different responses and reactions to similar or even the same events? Or why do I respond differently at different times to a similar situation? Something didn't add up.

The answer involves investigating the origins of our feelings and behaviours. Why do these pesky little things trigger us? Where do they come from?

THE CAR CRASH SCENE

Let's work through an example and explore our first scenario of an event or situation. I'll begin with an example of a car accident. Sounds morbid I know but bear with me.

There are three people in a car, let's call them Person A, B and C and they're involved in a collision. After the accident has occurred we notice that each person, who was in the *very* same car accident, has a different response.

Person A feels angry and storms out of the car yelling obscenities at the other driver.

Person B feels scared and stays in the car trembling.

Person C feels fairly neutral and relieved and calmly climbs out of the car to check on the other driver and to swap details for insurance purposes.

So why is it that all of these people experiencing the very same event, feel and react so differently?

There are a number of factors behind these different feelings and responses however the primary contributing factor is that of *our thoughts*.

Thoughts manifest as that little voice you hear speaking to you inside your head all the time. It's known as self-talk. It's a running dialogue or commentary and sounds something like this: 'What should I do now — maybe I'll go to Kim's place — I can't believe I just said that — I'm so lucky — What will I make for lunch? Mmm I haven't had beef stroganoff in a while.'

And on and on our thoughts stream throughout the day. You know this feeling, right? That endless chatterbox inside your brain.

What does self-talk do?

So, here's what happens — your feelings develop based on what you're saying to yourself about what has happened (i.e. the situation or event). Now, likely your self-talk will be different to everyone else's. After all, we are all unique.

If we take the example of the car accident, **Person A** felt angry and then behaved angrily, so we can presume he or she would have had some pretty fired-up self-talk or thoughts about what happened. Maybe something like, *"That bloody idiot! How stupid are they? We could have been killed!"*

Thoughts like these most certainly lead onto angry feelings and then they'll likely respond in an angry manner as well. Make sense?

Person B, who was left scared and trembling may have been thinking something like, *"We could have died! We nearly died! This is bad, this is very bad! I may never have seen my family again."*

Person C who stayed fairly neutral may have been thinking, *"Wow, how lucky was that? No one was hurt — what a lucky escape. Now we had better work out the next steps."*

Same situation, different self-talk. See the difference?

So on reflection we really start to see how a person's thoughts and self-talk has an impact on their feelings and responses.

The feelings we have are determined by what we think about the situation and what we tell ourselves about it.

In our example we have the extremes of Person C thinking how lucky they were to escape which made them feel lucky, happy and relieved versus Person B who thought, *we nearly died* — creating feelings of fear and worry.

Once a strong feeling is created our body releases chemicals which will cause our body to react.

For example, the thought, *we nearly died* and the resulting feelings of fear and anxiety could have physiological effects like increased heart rate, body trembling, jelly legs, feeling nauseous, tense muscles and so on. Following this physical reaction, comes our behavioural response. In someone like Person B's case it will likely be a response such as freezing which meant they didn't move from the car.

In the example of Person A, their fiery thoughts of *bloody idiot* are likely to trigger feelings of anger, which then triggers the stress response in the body, however the output or behavioural reaction is different because of the very different feelings of anger compared to fear. Therefore, the behaviour is more likely to be vocal or physical outbursts directed at the perceived wrong doer. So every thought we have can impact on our feelings, our physiology and our behaviours and actions.

HOW THE CYCLE KEEPS GOING

Imagine that you yell at your kids *(behaviour)*. "Stop pestering me, you little brats!"

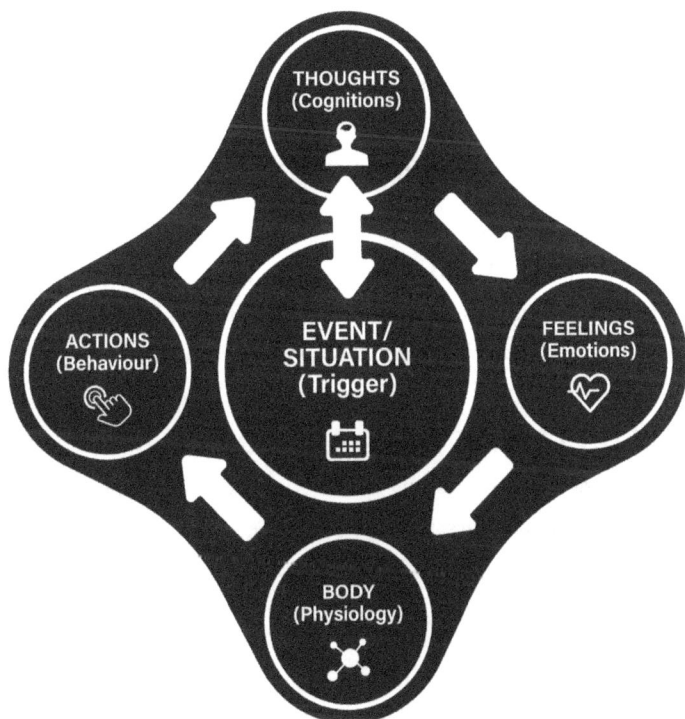

You then think, *I shouldn't have done or said that;* (a *thought* that will impact on how you feel). You feel guilty or bad about yelling and saying "bad" things *(feeling)*.

That guilty feeling will then impact on how your body responds *(physiology)*. Guilt can induce lethargy and reduce energy which then impacts on what you do *(behaviour)*.

This means you might start to withdraw or perhaps stay in bed. The self-talk says, *I'm hopeless; I'm such a bad mother!* From there, depression may be in sight and the merry-go-round spins faster and you don't know how to get off!

This is how the Think-Feel-Do Cycle keeps spinning in motion. Around and around and around!

It's important to know that this cycle continues on without the influence of the initial event anymore.

So while something may have occurred to trigger the cycle, the cycle continues *without* the situation.

The situation/event is a trigger.

And therefore we can know for sure that it's never about the situation or what happens to us that create our feelings: **it's the thoughts that we have about the situation or event that keep the cycle spinning.**

WHY DO I THINK THE WAY I DO?

From this new understanding of the connection between thoughts, feelings and behaviours the next question arises: where do these thoughts come from? Why do we all have such different thoughts about similar things?

Part of the reason can be attributed to the beliefs that we have about ourselves, the world and other people. Beliefs are tenets or convictions that people hold to be true, and are often formed from the experiences that we've had while growing up.

These beliefs can be influenced by many things:
• our interpretation of what's happened and why
• the stage of development we're in when it happened
• our ability to understand and interpret the world
• the existing beliefs and teachings of our parents or significant others in our formative years.

The most important thing to know is that we all have a different set of beliefs and quite often we're not aware of them or how they shape our view and influence our thinking. Unless we've done some introspective work on ourselves, most of us are completely unaware of what drives us and our behaviours. This is why, in the past, I had always found my behaviours and feelings such a mystery.

It was not until I started researching and doing the psychological work that I could start putting the pieces of the puzzle together. To finally explain what was going on, why I would do the things I did, and ultimately to understand I had the power to change my thoughts! Read on and you'll learn this too, I promise. It's friggin' awesome fun when you see how you can change your life.

BREAKING THE CYCLE

So how can this cycle get broken? I'd like to tell you about a client of mine called Narelle.

Narelle was a 42-year-old woman, married to Tom for 22 years. They had two boys, a 13 and 10-year-old. Narelle was doing all of the cooking and cleaning at her house and she was managing all of her kids' needs — school work, out of school activities, sports, and appointments. Narelle had trained as a nurse when she was young, and initially did shiftwork in hospital operating theatres.

However, after she had the boys, she moved into working part-time for the Royal District Nursing Service (RDNS) in her local area. This meant that she would work through the daytime and had more flexibility to be around and care for the boys. Although the work was meant to be part-time, Narelle often worked extra time each day and would stay overtime with some of her patients to provide extra care to them (e.g. make them a cup of tea or have a chat, or go and buy them a loaf of bread if they had limited food in the house).

Narelle also had ageing parents who had migrated to Australia from Italy in the late 1960s. They lived about twenty minutes from Narelle with very limited mobility, and limited English language skills. She was the eldest of two children, and had a younger sister who she saw infrequently, but talked to her on the phone once a week. Narelle had been the English translator for her parents since she was very young, and she was often at her parents' house at least twice a week to help them with their chores, medical appointments or other needs. Her mum also called her on a daily basis.

Narelle was referred to me by her GP. She came to see me because she was feeling very stressed, not sleeping well, and was putting on extra weight. She told me that she was feeling really grumpy, had lost her motivation and enthusiasm for life, and that she had recently experienced a couple of panic attacks.

When I first met Narelle, she was immediately likeable. She had a very dry sense of humour and it was evident from what she told me and how she was, that she was a very thoughtful and caring person. I asked Narelle how she would like to be and how she would like her life to be. She said that she wanted to feel happier, to be calmer with her kids, to exercise each day, to have some time to read.

After completing an assessment questionnaire, the results showed that Narelle had extremely severe symptoms of anxiety and stress, and moderate symptoms of depression. It seemed to me that Narelle was a highly empathetic person which often led to her being overly responsible (she felt constant guilt because even though she was doing a lot for others it was never enough). She had developed bad habits and unhelpful routines (all leading to exhaustion), she was feeling grumpy and resentful because in all of her roles she was constantly giving of herself (nurse, mother, daughter, wife) and there was no allocated time where she was giving back to herself or someone else was giving to her. She had high expectations of herself and had not been used to making requests of others or asking for help.

I explained the results of the questionnaire with her and explained the fight/flight response and the impacts of chronic stress. I explained how for some people it can lead to anxiety and panic attacks, and sometimes when stress is ongoing for long periods of time and/or very high it can sometimes lead to symptoms of depression. And that her symptoms of anxiety and depression were caught in a vicious cycle.

Feeling super stressed and anxious had set off her fight/flight response, and after prolonged periods of time, she became exhausted and depleted. I explained to her that we were not designed to constantly be "on alert". So when we are wired to fight or flight all the time we become exhausted, lose motivation or drive and become less engaged in life. It gets worse when we think — *what's wrong with me? Things will never be any different. I'm hopeless.* Which is exactly what Narelle was thinking to herself.

This type of thinking just made Narelle feel worse. *I feel sad, I feel hopeless. I feel powerless.*

Then her behaviour became impacted. *Narelle stopped exercising, began eating more and yelled at the kids.*

Then she thought — *I'm a terrible person, I'm mean. I'm lazy.*

Then she felt even worse — *depressed, anxious, angry.*

Then the behaviour got worse — *drinking too much alcohol, going to the pokies excessively.*

This cycle can go around and around like a sickening merry-go-round.

So we started to work on each area of the vicious cycle. I want to emphasise that this is an activity done in partnership. Narelle (or any client I have) knows their life and themselves way better than me. My job is to help people get back in touch with their resources and resourcefulness and then help them to take action and have a better life for themselves.

We first started with her **Physiology**.

I trained her in the 4-7-8 diaphragmatic breathing technique (to switch on the parasympathetic nervous system for relaxation, which automatically then switches off the sympathetic nervous system).

We discussed relaxation activities. These are different for all of us — for example I HATE sitting in a hot, smelly bath — not at all relaxing for me, but a massage — yes, now we're talking. Narelle had to find ways to relax and implement what she found relaxing.

Physical exercise — Narelle had to exercise at least 30 minutes per day – heart pumping cardio to burn off the stress chemicals that were running around her body and release her feel-good chemicals.

Mindfulness — We spoke about focusing on being in the present and knowing that in that moment everything is okay.

Limit anxiety boosters — because she was tired Narelle would have copious amounts of coffee and sugary snacks. Caffeine and sugar can increase anxiety — so we reduced her intake of these substances.

Sleep — We talked about establishing some good sleep practices. For example, only go to bed when you're really sleepy — catch the sleepy wave — you've got about five minutes to get into bed from when you first feel sleepy to catch the wave in that sleep cycle. Don't stay in bed more than 30 minutes if you're not sleeping and get up at the same time each day, regardless of how much or how little sleep you have had, whether it's the weekend or not.

Thinking area — We looked at the unhelpful thinking types and discussed her inner self-talk. We fleshed out the way she spoke to herself and whether she was helping or hurting herself. We discussed choosing a new story for herself and her life.

Feelings area — we worked on sitting with feelings, not trying to change them — just noticing, acknowledging and naming them, allowing them to be there or establish what you need to do. For example, write in a journal about how you're feeling without restriction — straight from head to paper without editing, have a big fat cry (put limits around this — e.g. for the next 30 minutes, each day in the shower for 5 minutes) and then engage in an activity. Stomp around the house or bash a balloon around with a tennis racquet, punch a pillow, sing out loud to your favourite songs.

Actions area — We acknowledged that behaviour change is important to get real change. So we worked on doing some things differently. For example: stop yourself from yelling or venting and zip your mouth so you don't do this and then give yourself a timeout. At times in the past, I have put my own hand over my own mouth to stop myself from yelling or venting — it's actually pretty effective. Tell people what you need and when you need it, don't keep going and think it will all be okay — this is how it builds up and can sometimes end very badly, for everybody. For Narelle, she knew it was important to give herself a time-out when feeling angry, and communicating this with her husband and kids.

Situation area — We looked at problem solving — making changes about the situation that she could change. Examples were:

- Boundaries around work hours. Narelle could pick one client that she will go the extra mile for that day and just do it for that one client. That way she could still feel good for helping but not overwhelmed or constantly short on time and energy. We had to do some cognitive work around her underlying beliefs and causes in order to shift her thinking about this, but we got there. Once work was finished, as she drove down the street, she visually and mentally "dropped the work and the patients off" so that there was none left by the time she got home. She also used music and singing out to shift her mood before reaching home.
- Engage her sister to do more care-work for their parents — have a conversation with the sister and tell her how she was feeling, what is needed and what is happening. Set up a roster with her sister so they share the workload of their parents, and communicate regularly about who is doing what throughout the week. This will help their relationship in many ways too.

Home life — Narelle was doing all the cooking, all the chores at home. We discussed calling a family meeting and making some agreements. She did a roster for cooking and chores and focused on how it could help them, what positives could come out of this for each family member? This way she felt it had a higher purpose and would benefit everyone, while easing the pressure on herself. In fact, Narelle started using this time to unwind, doing something she loved but never had the time for — reading.

- In addition, Narelle started using a Gratitude and Achievement Journal as a 10-minute daily activity. When doing this exercise, you write down three things you are grateful for. Small or big things, there must be three different things each day (e.g. I am grateful that I have clean air to breathe, a comfy chair to sit on, two healthy kids, my kind heart). And write down what you achieved today. Big or small (e.g. changed a washer in the leaky tap, put the washing away, walked for 30 minutes, helped a colleague with a difficult patient).

CATCHING THE EARLY CYCLE WAVE

The earlier you can interrupt and change something in the cycle, the bigger the impact, the easier it is to manage. It's really a simple game.

For example, if I can change the thought I'm having from "I'm lazy" to "actually I'm not lazy, I've been doing x, y and z all day. I'm just tired now. If doing exercise is important to me then I need to change some things so I'm not too exhausted to do it". If I was to say that to myself instead of "I'm lazy" that would likely decrease the negative feelings and therefore stop and change the vicious cycle. I'm also more likely to do some problem solving and work out how I can make it work for me. Not blaming, just being responsible for it, and then making a change that makes a positive difference.

Regardless of where you are in the cycle, making a change in *ANY AREA* can make a difference to interrupting the pattern and making a change.

I tell Narelle that the more areas we can make some changes in, the more likely the changes will be helpful and will stick.

We worked together each session to make the changes in each area. These allowed her to change and improve her quality of life and to reduce the stress and her anxiety and depression symptoms.

Some things worked and were very helpful, some things didn't work. When they worked we figured out how to maintain those. When they didn't work we examined what happened and whether it just wasn't workable or if we could tweak something and try again in a different way. Or if she just didn't get an opportunity to try it out (we've all been there!).

As Narelle worked on these changes she found that she was feeling lighter and happier within herself. She reported positive changes at home and that the boys were actually enjoying having some of the responsibility (not always, but she could see that they had some pride about contributing to the family). They were particularly loving being able to choose a meal and cook it for dinner (her job was to be okay with whatever the meal was and not judge or worry). When they cooked she had to stay out of the kitchen (her hubby supervised or did the cooking) and she read her books. She had also developed a closer relationship with her sister because they were now sharing more of the care of their parents, and needed to communicate more about managing these things.

She was letting go of the need to have a perfect house, and was exercising more, and this helped reduce stress and anxiety, which prevented her cycling into depressive symptoms. Her sleep had improved because she was practising good sleep habits, using the breathing technique, and exercising. With improved sleep and a reduction in caffeine and sugar, her anxiety symptoms were further reduced. And therefore, she no longer felt exhausted. Boundaries around the time she spent at work, meant she freed up some time for a healthy lunch and some reading.

By the end of our ten sessions together, Narelle said that she felt like she was back to her old self again, but a more improved version of her old self. We reassessed her stress, anxiety and depressive symptoms and found that she was now back in normal range.

Before we completed our sessions, Narelle had a clear plan for continuing to move forward in her life and ensuring that when some things slipped (which they inevitably do), that she knew how to catch them, and make changes to get things back on track.

YOUR TURN TO COMBAT THE CYCLE

So, where can you begin to make changes in this cycle?

PHYSIOLOGY

Think of your physical stress responses, can you combat the stress response in physiological ways that make you feel more relaxed? Exercise, massage, breathing techniques, meditation, swimming, warm baths, time out to yourself, bush walks, sports, playing outdoor games, running, Tai Chi, martial arts, playing tiggy with the kids, chopping wood, dog walks, home or online exercise programs, yoga.

THINKING

Become aware of unhelpful thinking styles (I have outlined seven of the most common styles in Chapter 6) and start to notice what you are saying to yourself. For example, if you are using a lot of "shoulds" in your language, switch it out with the word "could" or "I'd like..." instead.

Or if you are mostly noticing what's bad and negative around you, switch your focus onto some of the good or positive things — balance it up. Or perhaps you use language that is inaccurate and generalised, like — "He *always* picks on me" or "*No-one* cares about me"? Instead, correct yourself and be more accurate or specific. Such as, "Sometimes he says some mean things" or "It feels like Ben and Sam don't care about me". Then notice how it feels... does it feel different when you change it to more helpful thinking?

FEELING

Make it a priority to notice how you are feeling — check in with yourself on a regular basis. Ask yourself — "How am I feeling right now?" Name the feeling, say out loud "I notice that I am feeling X (e.g. sad, mad, bad)" (unless of course if you are sitting on a bus or any other public places, that probably wouldn't end well, so just say it internally to yourself). Then just allow that feeling to be there, observe it and get on with your day. If we can label the feeling, rather than trying to push it away or ignore it, then the brain knows that the message it is sending has been received.

Notice what happens to those feelings when we do that.

Feelings are messages and sometimes we need to uncover what the intention of that feeling or message is: there is something that we need to know. Ask yourself "What is the intention of this feeling? What is it trying to tell me?" Uncovering the intention may help to guide you to take different actions. For example, when I worked in corporate world, my feelings were definitely saying *"Run!"*

DOING

Select one thing you do that you know is not helpful and make a change to that one thing. Start small and just do one small thing differently. For example, if you're eating seven blocks of chocolate a night, cut it back to six blocks to start with. Then five, and keep making small changes until the action you're taking is how you would like it to be.

Or if you want, start by adding in a more helpful action. For example, you might want to start meditating or doing mindfulness exercises. Start small — start with 1 minute, or 30 seconds, something that you feel you can easily do. Then slowly build on that over time. If it's push-ups — do one each day for 5 days, then do 2 each day for 5 days, then 3 each day for 5 days...well, you get the picture.

It will feel achievable and you will build up to being able to do that each time.

I once watched a TEDx talk by a psychologist and behavioural scientist called BJ Fogg. He is the Director of the Behavior Design Lab at Standford University. He talks about how tiny, tiny changes made a huge difference in his life.* When I heard it, I could instantly relate to his methodology of making ONLY tiny changes first. I have often done the same as sometimes it's the only way to get started. He talks about trying to begin his tooth-flossing habit by just flossing one tooth! I know people who have started to get healthier just by drinking two glasses of water per day. Or walking around the block instead of trying a 5km run.

The change you make needs to feel easy to start with, especially if it is something you have struggled with doing.

This applies particularly when motivation is an issue, and in issues like depression. So start by making a small change, something that feels like it's pleasurable or something that feels like an achievement. It doesn't need to be something big, but something that fulfills that criteria.

Once you have done it, the rules are that you must CELEBRATE when you have done the action or task. And that means this — say to yourself, "Well done, great job. Good on you, you did it — yes!" and at the same time pat yourself on the back (yes, literally do it). And here's why — your nervous system, your brain, will love it. It will feel good. And then that will make us want to do it again. When we do something and it feels good we want to do it again, right? So let's celebrate more and do it for things that will help us change and move forward in life.

---

* www.tinyhabits.com

> *"Making a change in ANY AREA of the cycle can make a difference in interrupting the entire cycle."*
> — Dr Nat

REAL TALK FOR REAL CHANGE

- Situations or events may be a trigger but they are not the reason behind our feelings and responses.
- The way we think about the event and our self-talk creates the feelings that we have, not the event.
- The Think-Feel-Do cycle keeps spinning without the event or situation being present anymore.
- You can change the cycle by what you tell yourself about it. Change your self-talk, change your life.
- Make tiny changes and celebrate them like it's a festival. This will help us to want to do it again and feel good about it.

CHAPTER 5

TAMING OUR STUPID THOUGHTS
(IT'S THE SECRET TO LIFE!)

In so many ways our thoughts really are the key to the universe; our individual universe. You may not think they are the secret to life but they are the secret to the *quality* of your life — that's for sure!

It was an exciting time when I truly started to understand the process behind our thoughts, exploring a concept known as metacognition which means thinking about thinking. Metacognitions are the mental processes behind our everyday thinking; for example; planning, evaluating and making changes to your behaviours.

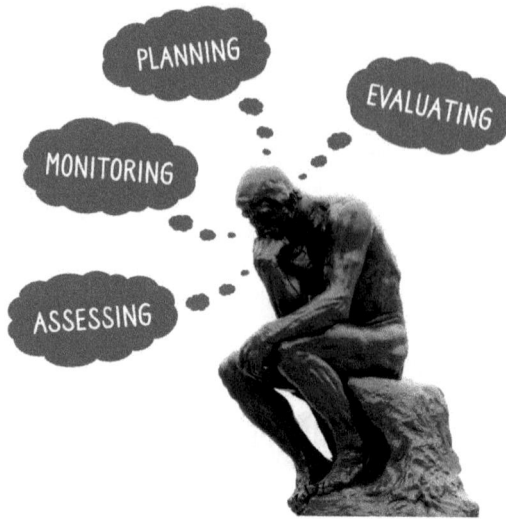

When I began to understand these processes, I began to change and improve my thinking and the quality of my life started to improve dramatically. So, how do we begin to use this fancy word — metacognition?

Firstly, we must begin to understand that continuous reel of inner chatter that can plague us all day — our thoughts. We need to see them for what they really are (endless streams of chatter) and find more helpful ways to deal with them. This will give you back some internal power and sense of control. It allows you to manage how you think and how you respond to your thoughts.

Thoughts don't have to plague you! They can be truly magical if you know how to use them correctly. And that's what we will go through in this chapter. Because if thoughts are left unattended, misunderstood or untrained, they can cause some mischief if we let them — they go wild and rogue and get harder to tame!

One of my clients Cameron once asked me — "Dr Nat, what is a thought?" He actually sounded more frustrated and annoyed than that, he said, "Geez, Dr Nat, what is a bloody thought? They shit me!" That's more accurate.

Now, this is a great question. Why? Because it shows me that Cameron was thinking about his thinking. He was curious to know what these things were that ruminated around in his head each and every moment of the day.

I like to explain thoughts in a very simple way. I describe thoughts as a miniscule moment when a little 'bing' occurs in your brain. Scientists would use terms like 'neurons and synapses firing', but basically they're little chemical reactions that fire off within your brain — *Bing! Bing!*

So why are there different types of thoughts? That's because the types of thoughts you have are formed in neural networks and based on different factors, such as your past experiences, values, beliefs, mood, associations and other chemicals within your body.

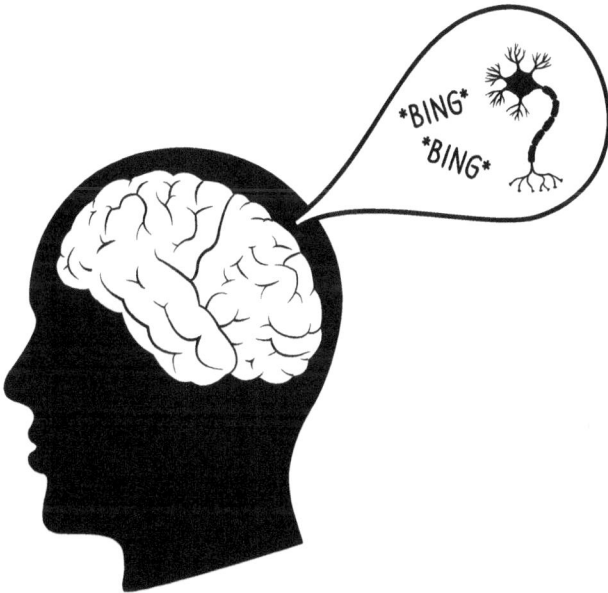

This little 'bing' is a chemical reaction, this chemical reaction = a thought. They fire off in your brain all the time. You have thousands of these each day.

Thoughts can automatically fire off thousands of times a day. It is very important to remember that just because you have a thought, it doesn't mean that it's the truth or even beneficial to you — it's just a whimsical notion — an idea being produced by the brain for consideration. It's a little chemical signal to say, *'Hey, check this out?'*

Thoughts are not concrete or absolute, they are simply little 'bings' firing off as we move through our day. Thoughts themselves are *not* the problem. Now I know it might feel like they are the problem but I promise you, they're not. They are chemical signals expressing themselves within you but they are not as powerful as you may believe.

Thoughts are only problems when we
relate to them as the truth.

Thoughts only seem insurmountable when we give them power by giving them attention and believing in them.

Thoughts are only problems when they're left unquestioned or unchallenged, and *fully believed in*. Because when this happens you operate as if they are a fact and even worse, a fact you can't do anything about. Which I promise you is not the case.

If we don't respond to them, if we don't *believe* them, then we don't act on them — then no problem, right? So, the next question would be, "But how do I know what is a true thought and what is not?" I'm so glad you asked.

HOW TO KNOW IF YOUR THOUGHTS ARE TRUE OR NOT

I have a surprisingly simple example I use to distinguish fact from fiction in regards to thoughts. You'll need to play along.

If I said to you, "I think you're a table," you wouldn't believe me, right? Why? Because you know that you're not a table. You might even try out the thought, 'I'm a table?' You'll investigate this strange idea to find out if there's any truth to the matter.

Once you've determined that it's not true, that you know you're not a table — there's no belief attached there and nothing to trigger further thoughts about it, it ends there. Period. It won't bother you anymore because you don't believe it and therefore you have no impulse to respond or react to it.

If I said to you, "I think you're a table" — the only thought you'd probably have is, *"I think she needs glasses or possible psychiatric help."*

ARE YOU A TABLE?

Now, keep playing along with me. Imagine if I called you a donkey. You might say, "Well I won't believe that either, I know that I'm not a donkey." And yes, most people won't believe it in the same way as the table scenario. However some nasty person could have once called you a donkey when you were a child and hurt your feelings. The word could have negative connotations or be associated with being an "ass" or being "stupid". 'Donkey' may mean a cute animal to one person or being stupid to another.

Some words can trigger childhood beliefs and for some, an innocent word carries a lot of weight and emotion, even if I just mean a humorous 'donkey' and nothing negative about it. It could impact that person's thoughts, feelings and behaviours.

Imagine if I said to you, "You're not good enough" or "you're lazy" or "dumb" — chances are this will bother you, especially if you've had some thoughts or worries like that already and especially if you value my opinion.

Now, here's the thing you must know: if there's a tiny ember of possibility or belief within you, you may start to believe it. And if you believe it then those words will have an impact on you. The more we hear and believe something to be true, the more it becomes a conviction rather than a contemplation.

You're a Donkey!

WORDS AND THOUGHTS

I'm here to say, that we are all capable of dissociating from other people's words and even our own thoughts, just as solidly as we dissociated from the thought, 'I'm a table'.

The truth and our thoughts are very separate things! As the old saying goes, *'Don't believe everything you think.'*

Thoughts only become problems when we don't try to understand the process behind how the thought developed in our mind.

They become problems when we blindly accept them as pure truth or facts.

The universal truth is that our thoughts actually go through more processing than the ingredients of a McDonald's burger! They are not pure. They are the end result of a complex process. Let me explain…

Thoughts are the result of a lot of internal and subconscious processing. Before they are even formed in our minds, the information goes through processes such as filtering, distorting and deleting. Now, you may think — why would my brilliant mind do such a thing? It doesn't need to delete and filter things.

Yes it does. It must.

You see, we are bombarded with literally billions of bits of information coming from the world around us, every second, and we simply do not have the capacity or capability to deal with it all. In fact, we can only consciously absorb about 128 bits of information per second out of the approximately 11 million bits of information we receive per second.

Could you imagine your poor brain trying to receive and understand 11 million bits of information per second. It would combust with information overload!

Therefore, our brain must narrow down the amount of information it takes in. So our brain quickly evaluates situational material by filtering, deleting and distorting the information received, cutting it down to more manageable chunks to process. Pretty clever really.

Nowadays, we are overloaded with more information than ever before, so imagine what our brains are attempting to do every day. This would also explain the rapid rise in people needing help for feeling overwhelmed and burnout. Because they are.

So, how does our brain know what information to delete, distort or filter?

It has to assess what is important. It determines what's important based on things like your values, your beliefs, your past experiences (memories), and even your mood to name just a few. After it goes through all of this filtering, distorting and deleting, our brain then interprets the remaining information which then become *our thoughts!* The things our brain has coded as 'important' according to our biased internal filter.

Considering the brain deletes, distorts and generalises based on those personal and individual factors, we never get the **whole** picture of something. We end up with an internal representation of the whole picture (like a map is a representation of a place but it doesn't have all of the information in it. It's why no two people ever really see or receive information in the same way. It's impossible!)

In fact, given that there is so much information, and so much deleting and filtering of information, and then so much distorting (e.g. generalising) and interpreting, I'm surprised that we can ever really communicate with each other at all.

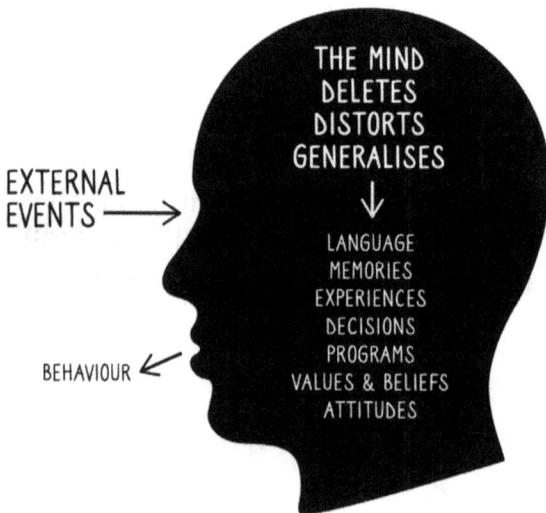

EXTERNAL
EVENTS ⟶

THE MIND
DELETES
DISTORTS
GENERALISES
↓
LANGUAGE
MEMORIES
EXPERIENCES
DECISIONS
PROGRAMS
VALUES & BELIEFS
ATTITUDES

BEHAVIOUR ↙

This explains why three people in a car accident will usually give different accounts and descriptions of what happened and what they experienced. A-ha!

Thoughts are the result of **a whole sequence** of processing and interpreting, so by the time a thought is produced at the end of all that processing, it is often *very* different to the actual facts or original information.

THE PROBLEM SOLVING BRAIN

Our brain is a problem solver, that's its job. So if we give it a problem, when it's operating in its peak state (and sometimes even when it's not), it will try to find a solution to that problem. It's quite marvellous at doing it. So if we have emotional pain, it says "that's my job" and it looks for all different types of ways of solving this pain. It does not necessarily always come up with good or helpful solutions, but it does come up with possible answers or options. It's like an over-excited helper trying to solve your pain or problem.

For example, sometimes our brain thinks that drinking alcohol is a good idea when we feel emotional pain. It may say, *"I could do with a gin and tonic right about now."* As some of us know, this is not usually a great solution. It can sometimes result in worsening one's mood and uninhibited behaviours that can lead to more pain and trouble, but in different ways. In extreme cases, sometimes the brain can think that a good solution, or the only solution, is suicide. This is not the truth of the situation, only that it's one possible option. It's just the brain's way of trying to solve a problem. It doesn't mean the idea is true, good or even wise.

It's imperative to remember that sometimes this combination of being in a lot of emotional pain and drinking too much, adversely affects our critical thinking capacities. Instead of resourcefulness, our brains bounce from one negative thought to another until it can end up seeing this as a possible solution. But please know — it is not! It is just a 'bing' in our brain that we do not need to listen to or act on! It is just an impure, highly processed 'Mc-Bing' firing in our alcohol affected brain trying to find a solution! And if you've ever been in pain and drank too much you may know exactly what I mean. (Cue cringing moments).

From this negative state of being, our brain will usually come up with some really crappy ideas. This is when we need to get help, some external help, and refuse to listen to the crappy ideas our brain might be suggesting. (If this happens I suggest you seek help. I have listed some supportive services and hotlines at the back of this book. Please reach out.)

Remember, these pesky 'bings' are only based on what the brain thinks it already knows and has experienced from our past and from our beliefs. Unfortunately the reality is, if these events were crappy, our brain will likely produce crappy beliefs and ideas.

It's a bit like the saying, 'Garbage in; garbage out.' When we experience harm or trauma, our beliefs can become really crappy, producing a cycle of negative thoughts, ideas and feelings. In turn, our physiology reacts to these stresses and our actions become negative by this point too. It all adds up, right? It can feel really shit.

I want to tell everyone that's experienced this negative state where our brain delivers us such shitty messages, to not listen to them, not act on them and ultimately to see them for the deception they are.

It's great to use this knowledge whenever a dubious thought arises — you can say to yourself — huh, it's just a thought.

Next you can ask yourself the important question; **is this thought helpful?**

Is this thought helpful to the way that I'm feeling or want to feel? (Not is it good or bad/right or wrong).

Is this thought helpful to what I want to achieve?

Is it moving me forward in my life, my relationship, my dreams etc?

If yes, then great! Keep the thought. If the answer is no, then it's a good time to check in and challenge this thought in order to get your power back.

You see, when we feel negative, we notice more negative and then we feel negative and the cycle continues. But that's because you have a brilliant mechanism in your grey matter called your Reticular Activating System.

THE POWER OF YOUR RETICULAR ACTIVATING SYSTEM (RAS)

Your **Reticular Activating System (RAS)** is a super sleuth. Its primary job is to focus on what you tell it is important. It's quite an incredible and handy little mechanism if used correctly.

Imagine it's like a spotlight in a theatre. You know that moment when everything is dark and silent in a theatre room before a performance and the spotlight comes out circling for the stage. The RAS is like your inner spotlight, it circles and tracks down things you tell it to focus on and highlight. So this can be great if you focus on wonderful things and it can feel like crap if you focus on crap. It's a very simple equation for the RAS.

So for example, imagine that you were driving around in your beat-up, old car and decided that it was time to buy a new car. You go into the car dealer and they have this very cute little green Mazda car, and you think to yourself, *"Wow, how unique, I've never seen anyone driving around in one of these. I'll be so unique and special driving this little car around. No-one else has one!"*

You buy the car, and then the exact minute you step out of the car yard, you notice a very cute little green Mazda car go past. Exactly the same as the one you just bought. But you swear you've never seen one on the road before. So you shrug the first coincidence off and keep driving down the road. Not too far down the road, you see another one. *WTF?! How can that be?* All of a sudden it seems that everyone is driving cute little green Mazda cars. But you'd swear, up until that point, you'd never seen one before — or had you?

You see, the truth is they were always there, driving right past you. But up until you decided that it was important to you (i.e. you thought they were cute and bought one), you never consciously took that information in. You never noticed it before then.

However, if we played the subconscious reels of memories back from your mind, I promise that there would have been lots of little green Mazdas on the road. They were always there, you just filtered it out because it wasn't important to you at that time. That's all thanks to the RAS. See by buying one, you've now told the RAS it's important to you and it needs to pay attention to that piece of information. And so, 'Voilà!' all the little green Mazda cars are now noticed because you told the RAS it's important to you, and they've all come into your consciousness now. How nifty!

THE RAS AND GOAL SETTING

The RAS is also one of the big reasons that we set goals. We're setting goals to help advise the RAS what we want. When we tell the RAS "this is what is important to me now" it starts to focus on things that relate to those goals.

For example, when I was looking to expand my business, I realised that I needed more consulting rooms. I had been working in one room at a local doctor's clinic, and had a thought and set a goal — "I need at least 3 consulting rooms close to the doctor's clinic". The next time I went to work, I was about to get out of my car, and briefly glanced into the rear-view mirror. Reflecting back at me was a sign hung out on a building across the road that said *Consulting Rooms for Rent*. I immediately rang the phone number on the sign, thinking I'd better get in fast, before anyone else sees it. When I rang he told me that the sign had been up for months. What?! I swear it had not been there before that morning.

Apparently, though, I had driven past it at least five times a week — for months! And I had never noticed it before– at least not until it had become important to me. Then it was like a neon flashing light. This is why it is so vital to set clear and descriptive goals. When you do that, the RAS will then know what you want and it will keep its eyes and ears open for you, and will bring into your awareness, things that are relevant to that goal. Things that you may not have noticed otherwise, just like me and that sign.

The RAS can also be retrained to focus on what's good, what you can appreciate, what is possible, what is positive, rather than what's not so good, what's going wrong, what's bad. The default of the RAS is to focus on the negative because this is what helped us all survive. If we were in caveman days, those who stopped to smell the flowers (i.e. focus on what's good) got eaten. Those who were alert and focused on what could go wrong (i.e. what's bad) — survived.

So we are from a long line of descendants who got really good at focusing on the negative. It's our default. Good for then but not so good for now. Now, we don't need to do that anymore, at least not for everything, and not all the time. Now, we really do need to stop and smell the flowers, be grateful, appreciate the small things in life, be in the present. In caveman days the focus was on quantity, nowadays the focus has shifted to quality (because we have quantity now). This is what makes life good.

YOU ARE AN INTERPRETING MACHINE

Our thoughts are the result of a lot of processing. And because of this processing we are then left with an interpretation or a meaning of a situation or event. Humans are super interpreting machines — we can't help it — it's our design. We make meanings out of everything.

It's been a great design, especially for survival in the past. For example, if I had witnessed Joe being eaten by a sabre-toothed tiger, then I would absorb this event and interpret it to mean that maybe a sabre-toothed tiger would like to eat me too; therefore, I should avoid tigers if I don't want to be eaten; a helpful interpretation of an event for survival. (Handy tip: you should still avoid tigers! They haven't evolved to stop eating us yet.)

However if we consider more modern situations, like every time a colleague seems to ignore me, I could potentially interpret that to mean that that person doesn't like me anymore. This is probably an inaccurate interpretation and unlikely to be true, and will likely result in a lot of negative feelings if I perceive (or interpret) it this way. However, it's what our system has been designed to default to: a negative interpretation.

Remember that all your interpretations have been through a lot of processing based on your past experiences, values and your personal beliefs. It's not the full view of the whole event; it is your interpretation of the event. Your filtered out and highly processed interpretation.

Interpretation, or looking for meaning, is something we humans cannot help doing, it's a mechanism to help us cope with all the information the world throws at us. It is not a bad thing. It is necessary so that we can operate more efficiently in the world. However, it's very unhelpful when we think that our interpretations of events are the truth; they are simply interpretations, not truth. So it's a matter of fact versus fiction; we need to differentiate between what actually happened and the interpretation of what happened.

Consider a situation where, 'Fiona did not look at me,' this is *what happened* (the event). Compare this to, 'Fiona did not look at me *because she doesn't like me*,' this part is an *interpretation* of the event or the meaning I've processed in my head. It's the story we tell ourselves about why something happened. It is not the truth.

We do not *know* why she didn't look at me but I interpret that to think perhaps Fiona doesn't like me. We need to remember this — **it is not the truth.** Even when we feel so certain it's the truth, it isn't.

All we do know for sure is, 'Fiona did not look at me.' We don't even know if Fiona ignored me, because ignoring is a deliberate action on her part and we can't know that. Notice that when we say, 'Fiona did not look at me,' it doesn't have as much of an emotional impact as 'ignoring'. Try it, 'Fiona did not look at me'.

Facts don't usually have that emotional pull because we haven't construed any meaning — it's simply what happened. It's only when we attach a meaning (she doesn't like me) to what happened that it starts to have an emotional impact.

I'm going to say that again: **It's only when we attach a meaning to what happened that it starts to have an emotional impact.**

When we fail to understand that there exists a big difference between what happened and the interpretation about what happened (our thoughts), then we start to merge the two concepts together.

YOU REALLY ARE GREAT AT STRETCHING THE TRUTH, JUMPING TO CONCLUSIONS AND FLYING OVER THE DETAILS. HAVE YOU CONSIDERED THE CIRCUS?

It can feel as if the story is the truth rather than a lot of filtered information that has been interpreted through our beliefs, values and past experiences to finally produce a thought — and there my friends is our very processed Big Mac thinking!

It's not pure, or reality or the truth. We can't let ourselves be trapped by thinking we know just because we think we know that person really well or perhaps because we think it's happened before — the truth is, we don't know — we can't know — there's just been too much processing from fact through to thought.

TRUTH VERSUS STORIES

Even if we put aside the processing element for a moment, it is important to acknowledge that we are not mind-readers. How could we possibly truly know the personal reason why Fiona didn't look at me? Even if Fiona tells me why she didn't look at me, I still may not know because she might not be telling the truth. Perhaps I will never know why. The only thing we can come close to knowing is the *facts* of what happened; the rest is a made-up story.

And it's fine that we make up stories; we can't help it, as I said — we're interpreting machines. However, understand that it is a story, made up by you based on all of the 'events' that you've experienced and interpreted before leading to this moment. Now I'm not saying that you make up events like J.K Rowling makes up wizards and wands, I'm saying that you believe your interpretation is true even if it's not. Why? Because it has come from your beliefs, past experiences and a whole bunch of other things — so you believe it's true. You believe your interpretation is accurate. Again, it is not a problem that you have these interpretations (they are necessary). The problem is when you believe that they are the truth. Knowing that you have made up the interpretation is what is most important here.

Knowing this fact can free you from the ugly grip these types of thoughts can have on you. Yes, you will still have unhelpful thoughts or interpretations but you will not be held captive by them because you'll know that the story is made up by you. You will begin to see these thoughts as just little bings in your brain; your interpretation of the event, not the truth.

To begin to become aware of this process of interpretation, next time you feel upset about something, ask yourself this question: *what did I just make this mean? What meaning did I make up about this?*

By asking yourself this question you are now interrupting the normal pattern of just accepting the story you're telling yourself about what happened. And you're bringing your attention to the idea that you have made it mean something; that you made something up. Even just doing this can be helpful. It helps to loosen the grip on what we might have otherwise perceived as "The Truth".

We have established that the interpretation that Fiona did not look at me because she doesn't like me is unhelpful to me and unlikely to be true. Then the next part of the process is to ask yourself *"could it mean something else?"* or *"what else could it mean?"* Could we then assume that there could be a whole bunch of other reasons that Fiona did not look at me? Absolutely!

The list of possible alternative reasons is long.
- maybe she didn't actually see me
- maybe she was having a bad day
- maybe she had something in her eye
- maybe her eyesight is failing
- maybe she was engrossed in what she was doing
- maybe she had a bad headache
- maybe she was worried and distracted about something
- maybe she's a terrible person
- maybe she was preoccupied with her own brain bings
- so many maybes!

Are any of these other interpretations a possibility? Yes! They are, aren't they? Now you might be tempted to say, 'Yes but I still *know* that it was this reason or that reason.'

However this must be challenged, how do you *really* know? Can you read her mind? Are you the world's best psychic? Are you Fiona herself?

Again, you may answer, 'Well no, but I just know!' It's natural at first to feel the urge to fight for your interpretation. As humans we like to be right and we sometimes feel the urge to do this.

But I'm here to ask you — what for? So you can continue to feel miserable?

What is being right about this going to cost you? What if you really could let it go and consider that there may be some other explanation for why something happened?

Remember we will never know the truth so letting go of the need to be right (in your eyes) could have you actually feeling happier. Wouldn't that be worth it?

Let's brainstorm some other interpretations or ideas of why Fiona didn't look at me. Then, let's evaluate these other ideas and ask ourselves, which one is most likely? We can review what we know about the situation or about the person. It may be something like this:

TRUE(R) REVIEW

- In my experience Fiona is a pretty direct person.
- We have been friends for a long time.
- I don't think she'd hang out with me if she didn't like me.
- I also know that our friend Jenny saw Fiona while driving past the other day and Fiona didn't wave to her and Jenny is a really nice person.
- I wonder if maybe her eyesight is failing?

BINGO! Now that's a real possibility. After all, Fiona is much older than me and that can happen as we get older.

Now we have a plausible alternative explanation based on some other evidence, and one that is more likely to be true and not just because it serves us better.

So how does this new review feel? In my experience a whole lot better! And remember the double whammy that you might be able to guess by now is that we're making all of this up anyway because it's an interpretation, just a story; it's not the facts. We may never know the actual real facts, but we do know the more likely explanations that have more clout or are more likely than your original made-up version.

So if we're making all of this up anyway, then my advice is to make up something that serves you better. Make up something that is more helpful to your happiness. And don't just make up some Pollyanna 'everything-is-happy-and-roses' version — that won't fly. It just won't work. Make up some real possibilities and explore them.

I once had a client Rose, who fell in love with a man. They had a whirlwind romance within two weeks and then suddenly, she just stopped hearing from him. No texts. No calls. Zero. She went into panic and assumed he was breaking up with her. In her mind he was ignoring her and had lost feelings for her. He had probably hooked up with someone else.

She texted him. No reply. She Facebooked him. Nothing. She felt rejected. She was in pain and beginning to grieve for the loss of their budding romance.

The story she made up was *her story*. Her interpretation of the event. The true story was that he had been in a workplace accident and ended up in hospital. His phone had been smashed and he didn't have her phone number. He was in no state to be able to find another way to contact her in those few days.

The truth was he had been thinking of her constantly and wishing that she could be by his side in hospital.

Now, her explanation for the event was plausible too as let's be honest people break up with others through 'ghosting' them all the time — but it wasn't the only possibility. It wasn't the only explanation available to her, it was only the one she was focusing on.

It's so tempting to believe that first idea or thought despite its distorted reality. Once we start to challenge the situation and check out some alternatives, there can quite often be a better explanation, a more likely or more logical explanation, than the original negative one.

Of course the old adage, 'if it ain't broke, don't fix it,' applies here.

> **If your thoughts are awesome and helpful and are working for you, in the way that you have the life you want, you're feeling the way you want and doing the things that you love — then no problem-o. Keep them!**

This technique is only for the thoughts that keep us stuck in a negative cycle, aren't helpful, leave us feeling shit and just don't work for us.

DO YOUR OWN TRUE(R) REVIEW

Be an investigator. A no-nonsense fact finding detective. What does the evidence say about your problem right now?

THE FACTS

List what actually occurred (not your interpretation of what occurred), this is the 'what happened' — what actually occurred and what was actually said, like a police report of what happened.

For example, I walked into my friend's party on Saturday night and another person that we both know looked at me and didn't say a word to me. No fluff, just the facts. Notice that it's not very emotion provoking. Just what actually happened.

....

....

....

....

....

....

....

....

....

THE STORY

Write down what you made it mean (your interpretation of the facts). Things that you have interpreted to mean something that did not actually happen. For example, *"I could tell just by the cruel way that she looked at me, that she was thinking that I was over-dressed and that I should just go home and get changed. I don't think she wanted me to be there"*. This is all just story.

....

....

....

....

....

....
....
....
....

OTHER POSSIBILITIES

Make a list of all the potential meaning possibilities. List everything else it could mean. What other possibilities could exist? List other interpretations of the facts that are likely or believable. For example: she had just got new contact lenses that day and she couldn't see very well so she was squinting. Or, she thought I looked amazing and she then felt under-dressed for the party. Or, she hadn't expected to see me there so she got a surprise when I walked through the door and was lost for words.

Have fun with this part — make lots of them up — they're all made up remember, even the original one you considered might be 'true' initially.

....
....
....
....
....
....
....
....
....

YOUR NEW STORY

Select one and have that be YOUR STORY.

Now select the most plausible/helpful explanation or interpretation to YOU.

It must be something that you can believe just as much, if not more than, the original interpretation or story you made up. It must be more helpful to you than the original story (remember you're the one who suffers from your made-up unhelpful stories).

For example, I'm going for "I looked amazing and she was under-dressed" — this is possible because she was wearing some old jeans and top, plus it makes me feel good about myself to believe that I look amazing, plus a few people told me I looked amazing — so I have some evidence for that idea too.

....

....

....

....

....

....

....

....

....

....

**NOTICE HOW YOU FEEL DIFFERENTLY ABOUT
THAT SITUATION OR PERSON WITH A
DIFFERENT INTERPRETATION.**

It feels better right? And with better feelings or emotions about something, we are likely to take actions and do something that is more helpful. Good, huh? ☺

REAL TALK FOR REAL CHANGE

- Thoughts are not the problem — they are only a problem if we believe them and don't challenge them.
- Thoughts are not pure, true, objective pieces of information. They are heavily processed interpretations and stories.
- Change the interpretation and it changes the feeling that results from the interpretation (thought).
- Negative thoughts helped us stay alive in the past. Use your RAS to look and find evidence for good. What do you want? Our RAS starts to look for what's great or opportunities to create something great.
- Re-direct attention to what is great and this will significantly improve how you feel and how you experience life.
- Check your facts, your story and the possibilities they each have.
- Investigate what you "made up" and made things mean.
- Select the story or interpretation that works best for you — what is most likely or most helpful, knowing that all interpretations are made up anyway.

CHAPTER 6

STICKY THINKING PATTERNS

Now, in my clinic, I come across some general categories of thinkers. We can all relate to at least some of them, if not many of them, at different points in our lives. But sometimes life experiences, or rudimentary thinking keeps us stuck within a mental framework and we become identified with our thoughts. We form patterns of thinking that we can't seem to break out of.

But I'm here to tell you that you can break free!

THE SEVEN STICKY THINKING PATTERNS

We have already explored the concept of negative filtering, which helps us find and focus on the more negative things in our life. Let's explore a few more.

BRAIN SABOTAGE

There are all different types of unhelpful thinking patterns. These labels include notions such as; worry; perfectionism or 'should' rules; negative filtering; blanket thinking; judgement; catastrophising or awfulising and dichotomous thoughts (extremes of right/wrong and good/bad). I've categorised them into relatable terms so you can easily spot them.

1. THE NEGATIVE NELLIES

The Negative Nellies of the world are often considered glass half-empty types. They are patterned to look for the negative before, and sometimes to the exclusion of the positive (and often voice it to others).

It's helpful to understand that Negative Nellies are most probably like this because in caveman days, they helped us survive. It was those of us who had the negative, scary thoughts and worries who survived. Being alert and constantly looking out for all of the negative bad things was helpful — we noticed when there was danger or threats around us. It helped us survive, so we are from a long lineage of negatively-focused thinkers. It was great — back then!

When there were lots of physical dangers, no-one cared about smelling the damn roses — it was too dangerous to stop and smell the roses; you'd be eaten. It was much better to be focused on what could go wrong, just in case. Over time and particularly in the last century of progress, our physical threats have decreased dramatically but our negative thinking and training has not. Now in modern times, focusing on all the negative things in our lives is not necessary or helpful. However, because it's been an inherent trait for survival for so long, so many of us still operate this way. They are the Negative Nellies of yesteryear.

Retraining For Negative Nellies

Therefore, it's important for Negative Nellies to learn how to retrain their brains and learn how to focus on some good stuff. They need to know that we are now safe the vast majority of the time. The problem is that our brains automatically want to take us down the path of the negative stuff that could happen. We need to retrain them.

So, if you're constantly focusing on the negative and bad stuff, you will get more of the negative and bad stuff. It's a very clever little brain, amazing really, and if we know this, then we can train it for good and not evil. We need to retrain our brains to focus on the positive and good that we already have and what we would wish for in our lives.

Remember, this good stuff is already there but the thinking cycle filters, deletes and distorts, we are not getting the whole picture — only what we tell our brain is important. Which is usually the negative stuff because of our survival instincts, and this is exacerbated because of the RAS. Then around and around we go — thinking we are dealing with the whole truth — that life really is shit and scary when in fact it is all a function of what we are focused on.

2. THE 'WHAT IF' WORRY WART

The 'What If' Worry Wart often has 'what if' swirling around in their head, with no answers, no resolutions, just increasing stress levels with every round of unanswered questions and concerns.

Worrying is different than problem solving, in which you purposefully address the issue with possible ideas, answers, and solutions in which to create a plan and take action. Some people feel that worrying is a good thing and helps them to be prepared. It's a way they feel helps them to cope, like they are doing something. This is untrue. All it does is raise stress levels and leave you less able to solve the problem. This is because doing this will trigger the fight-flight stress response.

Retraining your Inner Worry Wart

One way to retrain your inner worry wart is to set aside a specified time for worrying and put time boundaries around it. Then at all other times, you do NOT allow yourself to worry. When you start to worry, you remind yourself that it is not 'worry time' right now, but that you can do all the worrying you want, for example — at 7pm tonight for 30 minutes. If people are worried about not worrying this can be a good starting point for reducing the amount of time spent worrying.

You might give yourself two different times for worrying (e.g. 7am and 7pm at 30 minutes each). For this to work, you must be really tough with yourself and keep interrupting the need or want to worry, and delay it until the specified time. By delaying it, what can often happen is that by the time it gets to 'Worry Time', it doesn't seem so important anymore, it can be less intense, or we just don't need to do it anymore.

Part of the issue of worrying is that we ask the 'what if...' question but then we never answer it — so it's left hanging and it can feel very threatening. *'Oooh yes, what if it does cost more/get colder/run late, etc... aaargh!'* But really, just ask yourself — *'so what if it does?'*

For example, you ask yourself: what if I miss my train? Often we just focus on that and get all stressed about the possibility of missing the train. But what would happen if you answer the actual question.

For example, *'What if I actually miss the train?'* Then I'll get the next one.

'What if that train doesn't come?' Then I'll walk.

'What if it gets too dark?' Then I'll get my friend to pick me up.

'What if my friend isn't available?' Then I'll get an Uber. *Oh, okay.*

So basically this process is about getting to a point that you'll know you'll be okay, no matter what happens. If we answer the question then the answer is not usually as bad as it feels when we leave the 'what if' unanswered. This is because it's usually the uncertainty that causes the distress, not the certainty.

Here's another example: *'what if my boyfriend/girlfriend is cheating on me?'* Then I'll confront them and find out what's happening *or* I'll leave them *or* I'll be heartbroken but I'll survive *or* I'll kick them out.

See we usually know what will happen, and we know that we will cope or get support or figure it out — why? Because we have done it before or we've been through something similar before, or we know someone who's been through it before — so we know it's possible to get through, to survive, to be okay. We might not like it, but we will be okay.

The bottom line question really is — **will I be okay?**

And in most cases, the answer is yes.

And usually worriers aren't spending most of their time worrying about big issues, it's usually the smaller things like *"what if I miss my train?"* that consume all their time and energy and happiness. The bottom line and common thread running through all of this for worriers is — **"Will I be okay?"** and if we can get you to a point where you see that you will be okay, then the anxiety and worry will subside. And let's face it, with most of the worries that we have, you will be okay. How do we know? Because if you look back on the many things that you've worried about (and if you're a worrier you know there are thousands of them), things that you worry could happen, often don't happen. As Mark Twain said, "I've had a lot of worries in my life, most of which never happened."

What happens may not feel very good, or there may be consequences, but mostly it either doesn't happen or you are okay, you survive. And that's really all the mind and body needs to know, that you will be okay. Once it knows that you will be okay in whatever situation you find yourself in, it will stop bugging you with the constant 'what ifs'.

> *"Worry doesn't resolve anything in the future, and only destroys peace in the present."*
> **— Dr Nat**

3. THE CATASTROPHISER

The Catastrophiser is what we call someone who engages in extreme thinking. It's using language that creates feelings that are extreme compared to what the actual situation warrants. For example, I recently heard an advertisement for a popular cooking show. The preview showed one of the contestants baking a cake. All was going well until…oh no, the top of the cake had come off in the pan! They called this a *disaster!*

Now as logical and educated adults, I'm sure we can all think of a number of things that better qualify as a disaster. You know, like an actual disaster; an earthquake; a cyclone or miners trapped in an underground mine facing agonising death!

Come on — really! Look I understand, the media intentionally uses catastrophic language because it captures people's attention and leads to big dramatic feelings and responses — fine. But we must acknowledge this. It is a media tactic chosen because it creates massive emotion, and that's what we get hooked by. Fine for television — not fine for real life.

In real life, it is **not** helpful to use catastrophic language to describe something like missing a train. An example of catastrophising about missing the train might be, "This is the worst thing that could happen to me. I'll never get home now. What a shit show." Anytime you do this you will feel those big feelings and trigger a stress response. You will likely feel horrible in the pit of your stomach. Then you're unlikely to function at your optimum. Use catastrophic language frequently enough and you'll start to see things in a pretty negative way and create a whole lot of anxiety for yourself — and probably for others around you.

Another example of catastrophic thinking could be when you've got an exam you say to yourself (and/or others) "If I don't pass this test I'll be a failure and I'll never amount to anything." Or when there has been a relationship break up and saying "I'll never find another partner again, I'll die lonely and never be happy again." Anything sounding familiar yet? Even sayings such as "I've told you a thousand times" when speaking to your children about putting their toys away, or saying "I'm starving" when you feel very hungry or "My head is killing me" when you have a headache are all ways of catastrophising or magnifying events. It's not good for you, your wellbeing, or anyone else around you.

So I say here you need to stop it! Simply stop it! Missing a train is just missing a train. It is not catastrophic. Even if you consider the worst-case scenario, it is still not catastrophic. Do not do that to yourself or those around you.

This explains why people who have been through those really big events in life can appear to be more chilled. They have a different perspective from most on what equals a catastrophe and what events register on their catastrophe scale.

Missing a train or failing an exam do not even make an appearance on their scale of catastrophes. Yes it sucks to miss your train or fail your exam, but it's not a disaster.

While for some people, the way they speak and act, it seems to be a horrendous event on their catastrophe scale that they can't recover from; at least that's how their reactions and words present to everyone around them. It's just not good for anyone.

Curbing Your Catastrophic Tendencies

I'd love for you to just *stop it!* Yes. Curb this mind magnification behaviour. How? Simple.

Become more aware of what you are saying (either to yourself or out loud) then respond in a way that is more appropriate to the situation.

Speak calmly and appropriately to the situation itself. Use language that reflects the level of what it means when something happens.

For example, the top layer falling off a cake requires a simple, *'Oh no, that's a shame.'* Don't get sucked into the drama game to make everything sound bigger than what it is — only do this in TV land. In real life, keep it level and respond calmly. Place it on a catastrophe scale and see where it actually is!

Think of first responders, who could be running around screaming their heads off because they really are facing real-life disasters. But they don't do this because they know it doesn't help; it just makes it worse. Calm is the key.

One way to start to be able to put things back into perspective is to do a Catastrophe Scale.

CATASTROPHE SCALE

100% WORST THING THAT COULD EVER HAPPEN	**Instructions:**
75%	**100% =** the very worst thing that could possibly happen to you.
50%	**0% =** not upsetting at all.
25%	Start with the very worst thing that could happen to you, and work your way down to the least
0% NOT UPSETTING AT ALL	upsetting thing that could happen to you. In total you will rank ten things on the scale.

Start by asking, *what's the very worst thing that could happen to you in your life?* (You must be alive to tell it.) Some ideas or events that you could use to rank on the Scale could be: all members of my family dying in a car accident, a World War, losing all of my money, becoming a paraplegic, losing my job, my partner leaving me, my letters going to the wrong address, getting cancer, my kids being kidnapped, having a panic attack, not losing weight, forgetting my mum's birthday.

(These are some ideas to get you started and thinking. It's way better if you come up with your own things to rank.)

Now I understand that for some people, even just thinking about these things can be anxiety provoking. I get it. However, the end result is worth it. By doing this exercise you will be able to gain more perspective on, and rate, actually how awful or catastrophic something is. Given that many of the things we catastrophise about can often be very low on the scale, doing this serves as a great reminder that there are many more things that could be way worse, and the thing that happened (e.g. my footy team losing) is just an unpleasant thing, rather than an awful or catastrophic thing.

4. THE EXTREMIST

Welcome to the land of black or white. There's no grey. Only two options — black or white, certainly not both. This is also known as black and white thinking or **dichotomous thinking** where there's

IT'S EITHER BLACK OR WHITE.

nothing in between. The problem with this type of thinking is that it can contribute to emotional and behavioural instability, as well as interpersonal problems.

We see this when people believe there is only one way or the other. For example, there is only right/wrong or good/bad and they don't see that there could be possibilities between two extremes.

So how do we change this unhelpful way of thinking? One way is to challenge it. For example when you think to yourself, *'Oh no, I've done the wrong thing'*, my question is how do you know that you've done the wrong thing? Who's to say what the wrong thing is? What evidence is there for this? How do you know it's the wrong thing? I always call into question whether there is such a thing and how one can know. Usually it's just an 'out there vague kind of thing' rather than what you are personally saying. It's the same for good/ bad. And you can ask the same questions: How do you know it's good/bad? Who says?

Have you ever experienced a time where what feels like the wrong thing initially, later turns out to be the 'right' thing? Or it worked out even better in the end? It's certainly happened to me and made me reflect on my initial thoughts of it being the 'wrong thing' which actually turned out to be just right! When we begin to understand that there may be other possibilities (not just one way or the other) this is called 'being in the grey'.

Overall we can only ever know *our* interpretation of what is right and wrong in that situation. It is not the truth that our decision is the wrong one. It is our interpretation based on all of those things we are not conscious of most of the time (values, beliefs, past experiences). *It is whatever I say it is.*

Personally I have decided that whatever happens in my life is the right thing for **me**. Even when it sometimes feels very wrong, and can feel very wrong for some time. This is because I've decided that no matter what happens there will always be some learning that I can take. And all the 'wrong' things that have happened in my life have got me here, to where I want to be, without them, it wouldn't be the same. It just wouldn't be right. I do this because sometimes what I've considered to be the wrong thing has turned out to be the best thing. I just didn't see it at the time. Now I know this way of looking at things is not for everyone, but it has certainly worked for me.

Getting Some Grey in There

It's good to remember that we never have *all* the information (because of all that internal processing), so perhaps there are things we don't know that make it the right thing but we just can't know for sure, there's so much to consider.

It's really about understanding that there is no right or wrong or good or bad, only what I say it is. And really there is just a whole lot of grey in life most of the time. Being flexible in our thinking helps us to better maintain positive relationships, and be more balanced mentally and emotionally, which is good for everyone.

The main point to utilise for yourself is that whatever you deem it to be, it *is*. So if what you're saying is unhelpful for you, in that it's causing you great pain, upsetting you and preventing you from moving forward, then maybe it's time to consider a different interpretation. A different interpretation may allow you to change the situation, to problem solve in some other way, or to be more accepting of what has happened or what your interpretation has been.

5. THE OVER-GENERALISER

When you hear the words 'everything', 'never', 'always', 'all' — these words are clues that we are indulging our generalised thinking. It's also called Blanket Thinking or Over-generalising.

For example, you might have heard someone declare things like:

I'll never be successful
I always stuff things up
All men are liars
You can't trust anybody
You never take me out
I'm always wrong
I'm never good enough
You always use people

These are blanket statements that are very likely to be untrue. The problem with these sweeping generalisations is that they are often inaccurate and also very limiting. This is because when you think this way, and because you think this way, you're going to get what you focus on.

So you'll miss the evidence (because it gets filtered out or deleted or distorted) that shows the other side of this thinking. You'll miss seeing the nice guys because your focus is on the arseholes. Or you'll only notice all the arsehole stuff a good guy does.

You won't notice when you don't stuff things up or when things go well. Or if you do notice that you didn't stuff it up, you'll explain it away with some other reason like, "I was lucky". You won't let yourself own the great job that you did and feel good. Or your actions will be suspicious because you're so suspicious of others, or you never let your guard down with the right people and you miss out on making real connections with people. Blanket thinking or over-generalising is a strong wide set of beliefs that stretch the reality and make life a challenge.

Change Your Over-Generalising Generalisations

Over-generalising is often based on bullshit, invented beliefs or thoughts. If we start to use general language and thinking to reflect what we think is true, then we have a higher chance of having shitty feelings like helplessness and hopelessness, which often go hand-in-hand with this negative type of thinking.

Imagine if we were more specific in our language and thinking and instead of saying 'Men stink' I said 'Fred stinks'. This would not only be more accurate but would also allow me to be more open to other men and be appropriately wary of Fred. I would probably feel more optimistic about men, knowing that while Fred stinks there are still millions of possibilities that other men might not stink.

Even if you know 20 men or women who stink, that's still not *every* man or woman, not even close. You're getting the picture, right? It's important to be more specific and accurate in our thinking and language, to remain more open. Doing this then enables us to remain more balanced in both our emotions and our behaviours, making for a happier you.

So best practice is to be aware of your language and notice when you are making a blanket statement. Change it to be more specific and, in doing so, more true! For example, 'I always stuff things up', let's change it to what's realistic; 'I occasionally stuff things up'; or even better, 'I've undercooked the cake twice now,' (the more specific the better).

I loved changing these unhelpful and generalised words in my vocabulary. When you begin altering your generalised words, you'll notice it positively impacts on how you feel, and what you do — it's a game-changer.

6. THE PLEASER

Another type of unhelpful thinking revolves around judgement or being preoccupied about what others think. This is such a horrible trap in thinking and is what I call *mission impossible* and a fulltime job. Why? Because, as we've discussed already you can never ever really know what people are thinking, and secondly, even if you knew what they were thinking, you can't please everyone, and you can't please everyone *all of the time.*

Being a pleaser is rather exhausting because you're always at the whim of what someone else does or doesn't approve of, or more accurately what you think they approve of. You just can't please them all.

For example, if you're a fabulous tennis player, one person might think you're a show-off, while the next person thinks you're amazing, and another person thinks you'll never be as good as their hero Joanne — it's mission impossible, and it's just plain exhausting!

How to Stop the Pleasing cycle

As it's a game you simply cannot win — you may as well just please yourself. If you just please yourself at least you'll be happy, and you'll attract people who love you for who you really are. Plus it's so much easier and more joyful just being you. Simply doing this will reduce your stress levels by a spectacular amount!

Next time you feel anxious to please someone, or many, simply STOP and recognise that you're attempting mission impossible. Ask yourself which course of action would please you first. At the end of the day, you have to go home with you, and be with you 24/7 so you need to be okay at the very least, if not even happy, with your choice. Choose wisely!

7. THE PERFECTIONIST

Another unhelpful way of thinking is perfectionism or indulging in the 'should' rules. This thinking is particularly potent because most of the time it goes totally unnoticed and yet we suffer so badly from its effects. We will however, unravel the menace of perfectionism fully in Chapter 7. Yes, it deserves its own chapter!

But for now, here's a snapshot.

Perfectionism is often a silent epidemic ruining beautiful lives. It's the striving to be 'perfect', to live a flawless life. Perfectionists often have extremely high and unrealistic standards, which can be almost impossible to reach. A lot of perfectionists that I have worked with have an inbuilt desire to get their life "just right". And as we know, life isn't designed to go "just right", it's designed to go up and down like a see-saw. Perfectionism can often be debilitating because it holds us to impossible standards and doesn't allow for normality.

How to Depressurise Yourself From Perfectionism

To cease condemning yourself with perfectionism, it's important to realise that there is no such thing. What is perfect for one person is not perfect for another. The definition of perfection changes over time for the same person or within societies, and most people have never truly defined it, so they never know when they get there. And then, worse still, if people do get there, they find they're still not happy, and think it must be something else or they need to be perfect in some other way now. Nobody and nothing is perfect, you can only be perfect for yourself.

The problem with perfectionism is that you can never really know what perfect is and when you have it. How do you define it? It is so subjective. It's a nebulous creature that can lurk around many corners, never being able to really catch it. It's ever-elusive and as soon as you get "there" or close to "there" (wherever *there* is!), the goal posts often shift again, and you never quite reach it. It truly is 'mission impossible'.

Check out the next chapter for more on the juicy delights of curbing your perfectionism tendencies and understanding the 'rule books' in our head and what we can do to change them.

> "Perfectionism is a silent epidemic
> ruining our beautiful lives."
> — Dr Nat

HOW TO GET OVER YOUR BRAIN NO MATTER WHAT

I grew up believing something disempowering about myself. I believed that I was dumb. I was never told this by a parent or a teacher, it was something I made up (a story I had told myself) at some point in my life when I was very young. I think that it had to do with not wanting to go to school and wanting to stay home, so I thought there was something wrong with me and maybe I was dumb because I didn't want to go. Crazy right? I lived as if that was true for many years. I based my own self-evaluation on some thought I had when I was about five years old. And worse — I believed it.

Once I was older and realised that my thoughts were just an interpretation, without truth, but with a whole lifetime of processing, I started to honestly entertain the idea that perhaps, just maybe, my internal reality wasn't what I thought it was. Wasn't what I told myself it was. Maybe I *was* good enough? Maybe I *wasn't* dumb?

I started to look for evidence of this by either looking for it myself or asking other people I trusted and the evidence grew that *maybe* I was good enough. It showed me that *maybe* I was smarter than I thought; *maybe* I could do more than I thought I could; *maybe* I could have a better life, a wonderful husband, a great family. From listening to the evidence I started focusing on the good things around me, what I wanted and how I wanted to be. Then important elements of my life really started to change.

So the action I'm talking about from an everyday practical level, is to simply acknowledge a thought (that little 'bing' in our brain) remembering that it's only to signal to ask, *'Hey is this important? Is this something I need to pay attention to? Or is this something that I can let go of?'*

LETTING GO WHEN YOU WANT TO HOLD ON

When you know it's not a thought you need to pay attention to — *let it go.*

Yep, just let it float away. When you stop focusing so intensely on the thought, stop trying to push it away, stop responding to it, and just notice the thought and acknowledge it (e.g. 'Yep, got it, thanks for sharing Mind'), most often they let go of their own accord. That's what thoughts should do — just come and go. Not snagging in your brain for endless hours or years!

When we resist giving unhelpful thoughts so much attention, and redirect that attention on something outside of ourselves (e.g. watching a gorgeous sunset), we can just let them go on their merry way. They may pop back in, but that's okay too.

Just notice the thought and let it go again.

Sometimes it can help to make a picture of you letting the thought go. Some common examples of doing this are imagining that you place the thought in a helium balloon and then just let the balloon go, or put the thoughts on a leaf in a stream and watch it float away down the river, or imagining placing the thoughts on a train and then watch it depart and travel out of sight.

> *"Just notice the thought.*
> *Acknowledge it. Let it go."*
> *— Dr Nat*

The more often you can practise detaching from your unhelpful thoughts, the less frequent that thinking becomes a problem.

After a while, they can disappear or come and go without being a nuisance.

This doesn't mean to say it will necessarily disappear forever, but for the most part it should.

Sometimes, thoughts can reappear in moments of vulnerability or uncertainty, but overall they're usually at rest. When they do pop back up again, I just say, *'Oh that old thought/story again? Thanks for sharing.'* And I let it go, either refocusing my attention on what I do want or challenging the thought looking for a more helpful truth. I place no emphasis on it or put any emotion into it. I just observe it, notice it, then let it go on its merry way.

Especially if it's not a big hairy thought, or if it's a thought that I've worked on for quite a while using cognitive behavioural therapy (CBT) techniques for challenging and re-interpreting thoughts.

So it might go something like *'Oh yes, there you are again. There's nothing new here. I know the truth, and you are not helpful. Thanks for sharing'*, then I just refocus my attention elsewhere.

This gets shorter as time goes on, so it might become, *'There's that old thought again, thanks for sharing'*, then diminishing to, *'Got it, thanks'*, until barely a nod and finally disappearing. The less time I spend on it, the less focus/attention it gets, the better.

This is not ignoring or pushing it away. This is acknowledging and re-focusing attention. Having done the work I needed to, my attention is then placed on doing what is more important and more helpful for me. And after a while this enables the RAS to kick in and do the work so that it becomes more automatic, much easier to do. Good, hey?

PRACTISING LETTING GO

It can take some practise but it feels good to let go of thoughts that plague you. You can do this throughout the day. You can be shopping, making the kids lunch or going for a walk. You can do this exercise anywhere, anytime.

So remember, let's go through it one more time.

1. Notice the thought *(oh there's that old thought again)*

2. Acknowledge it *(thanks for sharing)*

3. Let it go *(let it float away)*

REAL TALK FOR REAL CHANGE

- Can you identify yourself in one of the Seven Sticky Thinking Patterns? (Most of us can). Remember these are just 'thinking habits' and you can change them any time.
- Look for evidence for where you are good enough, smart enough, funny enough, kind enough. You will find evidence where you direct your attention.
- You can detach from thoughts that don't help you. Just notice the thought and say, *'thanks for sharing'* and let it go!

CHAPTER 7

THE RULES IN OUR HEAD

Bloody perfectionism! I just don't get it. And yet at a whole other (human) level — I absolutely do. It creates more problems than it ever solves and mostly leaves us feeling like shit — and yet, we're addicted to it. We strive for it. We want it. We want our lives to be perfect and our kids and partners and jobs and homes and ourselves — all to be perfect. Whatever the hell "perfect" actually is!

Perfectionism really is the unhelpful philosophy of telling ourselves what we 'should' do. Those self-imposed rules that we find ourselves at the mercy of without ever fully realising it. Perfectionism has a lot of annoying 'rules'. Rules about doing the right thing, what we feel we should be doing, and questions like, "Do I fit in or am I doing the right thing?"

WHAT IS PERFECT ANYWAY?

What is perfect? How does it look? How do you know when you have it? How is it measured?

Even if you can define it, then is that what perfect actually is? Is it perfect forever? Or does it change, and if it does, then how do you know when it is no longer perfect? What has to happen to make it perfect again? Is it easier the second time around? The road back to perfectionism... arghhhh! What an absolute scam!

Yes, perfectionism is a scam!

A scam that so many people have bought into. We got sold the idea that perfection was real and that there was such a thing, and that we can all have it — if we try hard enough, work hard enough, not settle, not accept, just keep pushing — keep pushing ourselves, our partners, our kids, our workers.

But for what? To get where? Has anyone ever stopped and asked?

I'm not talking about goals or dreams here. I'm not talking about standards. I'm talking about some crazy pie in the sky idea (or not even an idea, maybe just a very abstract concept is more accurate) of being 'perfect'.

But have you stopped to ask yourself — what is perfect?

And even more importantly — what is perfect for *me*?

And why do I want it? What's so good about it?

What will it give me? What will it take from me?

And...what do I really want? And to what level?

And why? What is most important to me?

Let's pretend for a moment that happiness is really important to you. Then ask yourself — what needs to be perfect for you to be happy? Could you be happy without being perfect? If you are striving for perfection because you think it will bring you happiness, and then you realise that you could be happy without perfection — would you do it?

Perfection is about having unrealistically high standards. Did you hear? — *unrealistic*! That means they don't ever become fulfilled. Because they're unrealistic. That's the definition. You never get there! Because you can't. Because they are unrealistic. Plus it is about having high standards. Defining a standard and then judging whether or not that standard is high or unrealistic is all a subjective process. Subjective! Which means subject to someone's idea or opinion.

So who is it that decides what a perfect body is, or a perfect life? I have no bloody idea! But if you're going to strive for perfection, then you better bloody well know whose idea it is and whether or not you actually want it. And if you don't like who they are and what their opinions are, then what the hell are you doing?

My guess is that many people are trying to be "perfect" without ever knowing why, or what they gain or lose by doing it. Many never contemplate whose standards and opinions they're striving to meet.

SHOULDING YOURSELF TO PIECES

Most people that I meet only have a vague or abstract idea about what they think they "should" be doing. What they *should* look like, what they *should* have or own, what they *should* say or do with their lives. But they rarely consider specifically what it is they are striving for and whose ideas or standards of beauty, wealth, fun, they are trying to meet. It's just a truckload of insane *shoulds*!

Perfectionism can rip you off and cost you in a whole lot of ways that you may have never considered. We are often so blinded by what we think we gain from being or trying to be perfect that we forget to consider what it takes from us.

Here's just a few possible costs of perfectionism.

TIME

One of the biggies is **time**. It costs so much friggin' time to be (or trying to be) perfect. Think about how much time it takes trying to obtain and then maintain the perfect house, the perfect body, the perfect hair and make-up, the perfect kids, the perfect image (think about how much time you spend looking perfect on social media). Imagine if even half that time was spent playing with your kids, or out having adventures, and laughing and travelling and having fun instead. And that's just the cost of time.

MONEY

What about the amount of money we spend on trying to be perfect? Consider the thousands of dollars we spend on this! Just consider trying to be 'body perfect' — hair, make-up, beauty products, tanning products, botox, creams, diets, surgeries, gyms, personal training, clothes, eye-lash extensions. Then there's other things such as cars, houses, furniture, phones — always needing to have the perfect one — and for it to look and be perfect.

RELATIONSHIPS

What about the cost on relationships? Trying to make our partners perfect, or our kids perfect. How much time was spent fighting, upset, in distress, feeling unhappy — all because they weren't doing the perfect thing or being perfect.

CAREER

What about finding the perfect course at university or the perfect job, instead of the one that makes you happy and feel alive? What does that cost?

AND...we still don't even know who or why we're striving for all this. What the hell do we think we are going to achieve by doing all of these perfect things? It's rather strange, isn't it?

WHERE DOES THIS PERFECTIONISM IDEAL COME FROM?

These odd rules come from our survival instinct stemming back to our caveman days. Yes, those bloody cavemen again! Back then it was really important to be part of a group in order to survive. And we were less likely to survive if we got kicked out of the group. So in order to stay in the group, we compared ourselves to others and strived to do all the right things and follow the rules of the group.

We also learnt to conform when others in the group judged us so that we didn't get kicked out. It was a way for the group to keep control for safety and survival which all makes sense, right? For caveman days yes indeed. For modern life, it's far from helpful! It sucks actually.

Nowadays "the group" is much more than just a big family group, in fact it can really be considered as the whole world. We are all connected like never before. So when we start comparing ourselves to everyone we see in this enormous group, we will always feel we come up short. There will always be someone smarter, faster, better looking, more athletic, more successful, more caring, richer, prettier or simply 'more' whatever we're trying to be.

The world is a massive group, so now we'll never be good enough at anything — sound familiar? This unhelpful thinking links us back into the cycle of our beliefs affecting our thoughts and how we can't resist comparing ourselves and trying to be more 'something'. Good luck with that one. It's mission impossible!

Feeling not good enough compared to the group comes in a whole variety of forms. Here are some examples I've come across in my work:

- I should be thinner
- I should eat healthier
- I should go to the gym
- I shouldn't eat Tim Tams

- I should work more
- I should be married by now
- I should have made a million dollars
- I should be happy

The list is truly endless!

Talk about pressure! There will always be someone richer/stronger/prettier/thinner driving around in a more perfect car than you or I.

WHAT ARE THE RULES IN YOUR HEAD?

Each person's rulebook is quite different and extensive as well. Here's some I have heard over the years.

- I can't go to bed without washing all the dirty dishes
- I can't let other people see me cry
- I must be nice to everybody
- I must respect my elders
- I can't say 'no' to my children
- I can't take that new job
- I can't be happy if my partner is unhappy
- I can't enjoy Christmas
- I need to be successful before I can be happy
- I need to have all my washing done before I exercise

We all have some interesting rules in our head. What are yours? Have you ever stopped to notice them and question them? Can you list three?

1. ....

2. ....

3. ....

All these crazy little rules that govern our brain and therefore our emotions and behaviours with such little awareness can plague us and stop us living at our best. Even if we are aware of them, we assume they must be right and we don't question them. Even if we don't always follow them we still believe they are the right and proper way. When we don't follow them we often believe we've done something wrong and not surprisingly by now, we begin to feel guilty for breaking the rules! See the cycle?

YOUR RULES AREN'T THEIR RULES

Further to having your own mental rulebook, when others don't follow *our* rules, we get angry because we think they *should*. Even though these are not their rules — they are our rules — a bit weird right?

Our individual rules are not everyone else's rules. Really? You may ask. Yes, really! Sure, sometimes we share rules, but not always. When someone violates our rules — we can get mighty shitty. How dare they!

Firstly however, it's important to remember that these are *your* rules, not theirs. Even though you may feel strongly that they should be their rules too — they're not! Secondly, you are not the boss of everyone else — you are only the boss of you. You can have rules for you if you like, but you can't expect everyone else to follow your rules — they have their own.

Would you want someone else telling you that you have to follow their rules? For example, they tell you to only shower every second day. Not for me. So why is it okay to expect others to follow your rules? This expectation will also make life tough for you, adding even more stress to your experiences and relationships with others.

Finally and most significantly, these rules are actually made up. Yes, that's right — *you* made them up. This may surprise you but it's really great news because it means that you can change

REAL TALK, REAL CHANGE

them — anytime you want — woo hoo! How good is that! Yes they may seem inflexible at first having accumulated over so many years, and some of them serve you, or your family or community well, but when you become conscious of the unhelpful ones, they lose their permanence.

CREATE YOUR OWN EMPOWERING IMPERFECT RULES

When you become aware of your mental rulebook, you can start to evaluate them objectively by asking these important questions;

- Do these rules serve me well?
- Do these rules make my life better?
- Are these rules helpful?

You can take them one by one.

If your answers are no, then it's time to change the rule! Yes, change it! Give it a try — leave those dirty dishes in the sink overnight — see what happens…you'll see that *nothing* bad happens! Remember they're your rules; you get to choose. Leave the house without makeup? What happens? Nothing! Cry in front of someone, chew with your mouth open or whatever it is, nothing bad happens. You are okay, better than okay in fact because you have found choice and a new freedom.

It's good to acknowledge that these rules may have served you in the past, helping or protecting you in some way, but it's likely that you don't need some of these rules anymore. Maybe you can take some pressure off yourself and change old habits that cause you stress or don't make any difference to the quality of your lives. There may be consequences for not following some of the rules but there are important consequences that will affect you if you keep following the rules too.

Ask yourself which choice serves you better for the kind of life you want to live — the stress and pressures of following the old rule? Or the consequence of not following the old rule?

I would much rather deal with some crusty dishes the next day if it means I can spend more quality time with my partner and kids or perhaps get to sleep a bit earlier which also helps lower our stress levels.

How about this for an idea — maybe we could even make up different rules right now! Rules that help you enjoy happier moments more often. How about rules based on what is really important to you, your values in life, rather than rules imparted by Aunty Shirley when we were six years old or from watching our mothers follow their rules and taking them on as our own?

When you feel plagued by the rules in your head, you can ask yourself these three questions?

- Who says these are the rules?
- So what? What actually happens if I break them?
- What could I do instead?

TRANSFORM YOUR RULES TO CHOICES

Let's go further...let's get wild and change your rules from being absolute rules to being new choices.

What if you changed 'should' to 'could'?

Just that little change makes a big difference — try it now . Say to yourself, *'I should go to the gym'* and notice the heavy feeling it creates. Now say, *'I could go to the gym'* and notice how that feels lighter.

From finger-pointing and pressure arising from the word 'should', the word 'could' gives you a vision of balance and choice which feels much better.

And here's the truth; it *is* a choice.

You don't have to go to the gym. The only thing we all really have to do is die at some point — all the rest is a choice. From brushing our teeth every night to even paying taxes, it's a choice. Of course there are always consequences for our choices, but we do have choice.

Even when it seems like we don't have a choice, reminding ourselves that we do can be very helpful. When I remember that I have a choice to go to the gym it feels a lot better, I'm more likely to actually go, and go along with more joy. Especially when I base my choice on the fact that health is an important value to me and I am not just thinking that I 'should' do it.

When I choose not go to the gym then I don't ride the guilt-trip or feel bad. And no, this is not dangerous — in fact it's really good. When I feel okay with my decision not to go and there are no bad feelings associated with that then I'm more likely to want to work out another day. See how that all works? Weird but great, hey?

When we remind ourselves that we have choice, then we are more likely to consider and evaluate calmly and make a more powerful decision. For example, I don't mind admitting that saying 'I should go to the gym' makes me feel a bit cranky and rebellious and not want to go at all. My childish, you-can't-make-me streak comes out.

However, when I say to myself, 'I could go to the gym tonight', I like that so much better. I weigh things up and I ask myself, 'What is most important to me? What values would I be forwarding? How will I feel when I go? What is it that going to the gym will give me?' I am able to make a choice more powerfully because in reality, it may be that actually going to the gym will not benefit my health at that moment if I have an injury and am supposed to be resting. Or perhaps it will go against a more important value such as family and it's my child's birthday dinner that evening.

So the great thing about understanding choice is that when I say *no*, I am clear about why, and then I don't feel guilty. On top of that, I am more likely to consider rescheduling because health is important to me and my goal is to get fit, so I ask myself honestly, 'When could I go next?' Try it out and see how different that feels. You can go to your child's birthday dinner without guilt, knowing that you are still meeting your needs.

Now, if I do say *yes*, rather than being resentful and grumpy about going (because I *should*), I am clear as to why I have chosen to go, and I am likely to go with more joy and excitement and to be more focused on the workout. This leaves me empowered and excited about going to the gym, and I will be more likely to go again. This breaks the cycle of feeling forced to go or rebelling and not going then feeling guilty, and then eating lots of birthday cake and maybe not going again because you feel bad and depressed and unmotivated now.

Now I'm not saying you need to go through all this checking and questioning every time — but it will help create a useful habit. So even when the gym is in your schedule and you have it as a must — you can stop, remind yourself, and choose the option that works best for you (and sometimes you won't, but that's okay, too). Know your why!

YOUR WHY IS NOT THEIR WHY

When you feel you SHOULD do something, my question for you is, *'Who says?'* *Who says that you 'should' do these things?*

Part of the answer is likely to come from comparing yourself to the 'group', and the other part most certainly comes from the rulebook that we carry in our heads. Sure, this unique set of rules probably developed over the many years you've been alive and has accumulated from many different people and sources. The most common contributors to this rulebook are parents, teachers, friends, experiences, partners and so on.

For example, one rule you might follow is to never leave the house without wearing makeup. You just know this rule, it was subtly instilled in you somewhere along the way and you follow it — it's just how it is and you've probably never considered not doing it. You have to brush your teeth each night too, don't you? You simply wouldn't not do it. That would be terrible, right?!

ORIGINAL YOU

But while we are busy breaking old rules, here's another crazy thought — what if you started being original? Just being YOU!

You not only broke old rules that no longer work for you but you began to create your own ideas and concepts of what is "perfect" for you?

What if you decided what brought you happiness and joy?

What would feeling alive and excited be like for you?

What if you realised that all this crazy *shoulding* was based around acceptance and connection and love and joy and happiness.

What if, at the bottom of perfectionism, the real longing and wanting of being perfect was to feel accepted and loved and connected and happy?

And what if you could have this without being perfect?

That you could get it by living a life that was designed by you, for you. Holy shit! What a bloody relief.

"You mean, I could get what I want without spending all of that time and money, and without being upset and unhappy and distressed, striving for standards defined and set by someone else?"

YES!

"You mean to tell me that I can give up the notion of perfection and striving for it?"

YES!

"Well sign me the hell up!"

Here's the real talk: bottom line is, mostly, we all just want to be loved and connected and to be accepted and happy. Thinking that perfectionism is the way to get this is bullshit. The way to get this is to set your own standards and **make progress — not perfection**.

Making realistic, exciting, fun, amazing, challenging, inspiring standards that thrill you. Ones that light you up and don't take you away from what is most important to you but move you towards what you want. This will get you what you truly want, what we all want, and perfectionism is not the way to this.

REAL TALK FOR REAL CHANGE

- Perfectionism is a scam! Don't get trapped by its fraudulent ways. Make your own rules that don't revolve around "shoulding" yourself to pieces. Ask, *'what is perfect for me?'* rather than *'is this perfect?'*
- Remember that other people may have different 'rules in their head' than you do and that's okay.
- Transform your rules to choices by changing 'should' to 'could'. I *could* go to the gym is much more empowering than I *should* go to the gym.

Dr Nat is sharing more in her INTERACTIVE book.

See exclusive behind-the-scenes videos, audios and photos.

DOWNLOAD it now at **deanpublishing.com/realtalk**

CHAPTER 8

BREAKING UNHELPFUL BELIEFS

I once had a client called Peter. Peter believed he wasn't a good father. He worked too much and got home late. He was always exhausted and never had extra time to be with his kids. He had become the replica of his own workaholic father and had formed a belief that he was a "bad father".

The truth was he wasn't a bad father. He didn't smack his kids or yell and criticise them like his dad had done to him. When Peter was about six, he asked his dad to play with him. His dad said, "I don't have time to play, I am too busy earning money to feed you and keep you clothed. That's more important."

Peter ran that idea in his mind as a young child and learned to believe that money was more important than time. He felt that it was his fault that his dad couldn't play with him. He believed that dads couldn't play because they worked so hard, and because of all of this, he was a bad father.

Over time, as Peter and I worked together, he began to see that his belief wasn't true. We examined the evidence of what a good or bad father would do or be, and he began to see that perhaps he wasn't such a bad father after all. He also began to realise that working dads could have a balanced life. They could earn money and play with their kids. We worked through Peter's unhelpful beliefs, examining and challenging them and put some strategies together. Peter now does both. He balances his time well between family and work and believes he is "a good dad".

You see, Peter became aware of his beliefs and investigated them. He took a good hard look at what he believed and questioned their validity. He asked himself things like:

What are my beliefs about being a father?

What do I believe a "good dad" and a "bad dad" do/act/say?

Are my beliefs actually true?

Are my beliefs true for me now?

ONE OF THE BIGGEST FACTORS TO INFLUENCE OUR THOUGHTS

The biggest factor to influence our thoughts are the beliefs that we hold. Beliefs about ourselves, other people and the world around us. Beliefs about anything and everything really.

What we believe influences the way that we think.

So not so surprisingly — crappy, unhelpful beliefs lead to unhelpful thoughts, feelings and behaviours.

If you have a belief that "everyone is untrustworthy", then this will influence how you think when something happens. For example, if you go out with people you don't know very well and suddenly realise that you can't find your phone! Your immediate thought may be that someone in that group stole your phone — based on your belief that you can't trust anyone.

Thinking that someone stole your phone will arouse feelings of suspicion, anxiety or anger. These feelings then influence your physiology and force your body into a stress response, which then impacts your behaviour. See the cycle starting to wind up and around?

You may then start to question people or try to peek into people's bags (which will raise a few eyebrows!). Yet all your behaviours are based on a belief you probably developed a long time ago, that "everyone is untrustworthy." And maybe you just left your phone in the car or at home!

Of course, the opposite can also be true. You can have a belief that "people are trustworthy" and when you lose your phone you may assume that some good citizen will most likely hand it in.

One person can believe it's stolen based on their unconsciously learned beliefs and another may think it will most likely be handed in by a Good Samaritan. The beliefs we have influence the way we perceive a situation, an event or a person. Quite powerful really.

PIVOTAL MOMENTS IN OUR LIFE

So the big question is where do we get our beliefs? I'm glad you asked.

Our beliefs develop from a number of sources; past experiences, our ancestors and familial identity, significant others like teachers or parents, cultural practices or from the survivor mentality we developed.

A common foundation for many adult beliefs is the interpretations we made when we were growing up. Our younger selves made unconscious decisions that formed beliefs while our brain was still immature and developing. For example, that time that Dad forgot to pick you up at soccer training when you were 10. In that moment your brain looks for an explanation and decides it must be because he doesn't care about you. You then form a belief 'no-one cares about me'. Over time you collect one-sided evidence (not consciously but unconsciously), to support your unhelpful belief that 'no-one cares about me'. So anytime something happens that could be interpreted as no-one cares about me, you hold onto that evidence, and then your brain says *'see I was right, no-one actually cares'*.

By the way, our brain loves to be right about things! This is why so often we hold onto our beliefs, even when we have evidence to the contrary. Often we want to prove ourselves right even if our beliefs don't help us move forward in our life in any way.

Often there can be pivotal moments or events that occur as we grow up that cause our beliefs to solidify. We can find these pivotal beliefs resurfacing at certain ages or times in our lives.

For example, a young person who has been sexually abused may develop relationship/sexual issues in their adult years.

I often use this example with my clients — if something significant happened when I was five years old, which I *interpreted* without examination to form a belief, then I could well become a 50-year-old woman living through the belief of a five-year-old. (I am using this example because this is what happened to me). An early incident when a teacher scolded me harshly and said "You'll never amount to anything!" became the trigger moment for forming a belief about my intelligence. At that innocent and formative age, with the brain development and maturity and understanding of a five-year-old, I decided that meant, "I am dumb".

Now remember, this is the language of a five-year-old. So what happens is that my developing brain starts to look for evidence of this to see if it's true or not. This is where the Reticular Activating System (RAS) springs into action and starts highlighting the evidence of what we believe in.

So if you begin to believe that you're dumb, your RAS will find evidence of it, no matter how small or inconsequential. It's also not helped by the fact that we can interpret events any way we like. So even if something happens that's not about you being dumb, your brain can still twist and interpret it in a way that appears like you're dumb — therefore having more evidence. Now of course, your brain will like that because you get to be right, even if it sucks.

Now when this happened to me, the evidence in my mind began to mount and I started to see evidence of it everywhere. And that's exactly what happens to all of us. Little beliefs begin to grow and form what we consider "a truth". As humans, we like to prove ourselves right, so we keep finding evidence for our beliefs regardless of whether they're actually true or not. Finding evidence only makes your beliefs stronger and stronger. Until that belief becomes like a fortress wall in front of your own eyes, so high and deep and impenetrable that you can't see over it or through it.

And if and when you do come across any evidence that indicates that you might just be intelligent, then you explain it away as being some chance or anomaly. For example, if you get an 'A' on an assignment, you may think or say *"that's just because they made it easy"* or *"everyone got an A, it's not because I'm smart or anything"*. You win a prize for being the best student in Maths — you say *"it was because lots of smart people were away that day"*.

Now if I carry a belief that 'I am dumb,' I may also act in accordance with this belief. I may not even attempt to do things that smart kids do. I may classify myself into 'the dumb class'. Or not attempt to play trivia games or do crosswords.

I now become so embarrassed and upset about this belief that I don't want anyone to find out the 'truth' about me being dumb. My dirty little secret. So I'll do my very best not to let anyone find out that I'm dumb, all the while believing that I am, and that any day I will be found out. It can feel like a continual anxiety that hums along inside your brain and body.

In actual fact, I am likely to be pretty smart because I've worked hard so that no-one finds out my secret 'truth'. My problem however grows as I can't understand or acknowledge this even to myself. I feel like a fraud, an imposter. I become anxious that any day someone is likely to discover how dumb I really am. My secret will be exposed.

This happens to all of us and quite often it's hard to identify what is running our underlying fears and anxieties.

Does any of this sound familiar? Do you have a hidden belief, and worry that people may find out?

> *"Beliefs feel true even if they're factually not. It seems like we simply have so much evidence for these beliefs, we consider them as facts."*
>
> **— Dr Nat**

When we learn to look at all the evidence with objectivity, what we often find is the opposite of the belief we've held. However because this conditioned belief is so ingrained in our psyche we often feel convinced that it's true (plus we like being right about things, right? Crazy!) so without even realising it, we start to fight for our shitty beliefs — *"no, no, you're wrong, I really can't do that; I'm not smart."* Our behaviour stems from our beliefs and because we feel that it's so "normal" to us, we often never question it. Does this make sense?

We can be unconscious of our own beliefs so we don't question them.

Being unconscious of our beliefs means that we can go through our lives living with the beliefs we formed when we were five-years-old and feeling as though they really are true. When in actual fact it's some idea that we came up with to explain why something happened or why someone said something to our immature, developing five-year-old brain! We can carry this formed belief around for the rest of our lives if we don't question them.

Once we become conscious of our beliefs, we can question them and examine if they are *really* true.

For example, if I am a member of the high IQ society of Mensa can I still be considered dumb? If my brain still holds this 'dumb' belief it will want to justify it and say; *'Well Mensa must have had an easy test that year'* or *'I must have slipped through the cracks'* or *'I'll be found out any day now'*, or *'They made a mistake'* or *'It was just a fluke'*.

It tries to find an explanation on why you're still actually dumb despite the fact you are in Mensa.

So, what do you do?

You must challenge this belief and find evidence to the contrary.

I had to look at myself objectively when this happened to me. I found evidence and said to myself 'Ok Natasha. You have four university degrees, including a doctorate now — can you still be considered dumb with all of that when only a very small percentage of the population holds these degrees?'

I know this may seem crazy to you, but the brain can do this. It can still hold a belief despite the evidence. So, it's your job to challenge your beliefs. No one can give you a new belief on a platter.

You must look at all the evidence (balanced on both sides), and investigate if it's just a shitty belief that you made up when you were five years old, or seven or ten.

Yes, you heard me correctly — *Made up!* It wasn't even true. It was the best you could come up with as a five-year-old to explain what happened. How can you blame that child for doing their best with the knowledge that they had at the time?

Do you want to live the rest of your life through a decision that you made when you were five? I know some five-year-olds and I do not want to live through a five-year-old's decision — not for me, thanks! No sir-eee! I have outgrown my need to wear princess costumes and to believe I'm not smart. (Okay, maybe I haven't outgrown all princess costumes but you get my point).

So...what do we do? It's time to finally accept that at least some of your conditioned beliefs are not true, probably never were, and you may have lived for 45 years as if they were true — what a bummer! But you don't have to keep living that way now. No way hozay! Life is for living. Life is for reinvention and evolution.

So, what should we do?

Look for new evidence for the other side of the belief that you have been filtering out.

We do this now with the conscious knowledge that this idea or belief was something you made up when you were young, and with consideration that it may not be true. We do it with some doubt about the validity of this belief now.

Look for evidence of you being smart; or talented, or kind or a good partner. Whatever it is for you.

Consider all the moments in your day when you have evidence for the beliefs you've been trying to filter out.

For example, the "I am dumb" belief. Look for evidence during the day when you've been smart. You could also take a test, consider some activities that you're comfortable with and compare your results with average people or test scores, they're readily available online nowadays.

Or ask some friends who you know will tell you the truth. Really investigate and see if there is evidence to the contrary. When you really look, my bet is you will find evidence for both sides. In many things, when we actually look, we can usually find evidence for both sides of any story or belief that we have.

CHANGE YOUR BELIEFS, CHANGE YOUR STORY

What do you believe about yourself?

What do you believe about the following: Finish the sentence to reveal some of your beliefs...

Money is

....

....

Family is

....

....

Health is

....

....

Happiness is

....

....

Relationships are

....

....

Love is

....

....

My career/work is

....

....

My skillset is

....

....

My character is

....

....

I am

....

....

People are

....

....

The world is

....

....

What childhood beliefs are you still living through?

....

....

....

....

....

....

....

....

....

....

....

....

....

....

....

With the idea that you may be wrong, find evidence to the contrary (opposite belief).

....

....

....

....

....

....

....

....

....

What is the most likely truth?

....

....

....

....

....

....

....

....

....

....

CREATE YOUR NEW STORY

Make up a new story based on your new findings. That perhaps you aren't dumb after all, that perhaps you are more intelligent than you first thought.

Make up a new belief or story that better serves you. A more *likely* story that will really light you up. Create a belief that means you think new and better thoughts, and therefore feel a new and better way, which then means a better impact on your physiology and behaviour.

Now remember your new story doesn't have to be the *exact opposite* of what your old story was (e.g. I was dumb but now I am smart or I was untrusting now I trust everybody).

Break it down into positive reasonable details, something like this, 'I am resourceful, hard-working, and make good decisions'. Or I am 'discerning and intelligent with my decisions about trust'.

Imagine having these beliefs instead! They are balanced and heading you in a positive direction.

Would you react differently with this belief if you lost your phone? Would you still be wanting to frisk all of your new friends? Or would you be retracing your steps and using problem solving skills to work out what happened in a calm, resourceful way? So much better!

When we change our story, does it mean that we never do dumb things or make poor decisions? Of course not! We all do. But changing our story allows us to see the whole picture, in a more balanced way. Choosing different stories often leads to healthier and better outcomes. Pretty cool, hey?

You don't have to be stuck living out an old story that no longer works for you.

You can reinvent yourself by reinventing your beliefs! It's magic when you try. Let's give it a shot. Challenge a disempowering belief and rewrite your new story.

WRITE YOUR NEW STORY

Write your new story down. Yes, take a pen and begin to mark your new chapter.

What are the new beliefs that you would like to hold?
If you held these new beliefs, how would you act?
What self-talk would you have?
How would you feel?

....

....

....

....

....

....

....

....

....

....

....

....

....

....

....

REAL TALK FOR REAL CHANGE

- Beliefs are just stories that we made up and then lived as if they were the truth.
- We can challenge the belief by considering that it may not be true and then broadening our examination of the evidence we have for that belief.
- We can make up a new story or belief that is more helpful and more 'true' for the kind of life we want to live.

CHAPTER 9

BLOODY EMOTIONS! BLOODY STRESS!

Emotions — bloody emotions! I know, I know, they are important, but they sure can create havoc if we let them. However just like thoughts, they are not in charge. They are a little chemical message or a little bing! An alert sent to our body from our brain that says, *'Hey, check in on this thing will you? I'm just not sure but there's possibly something here that you may need to pay some attention to'.*

Emotions are part of our internal system that communicates different messages to us.

That's all they technically are. Emotions can be both amazing and tough to deal with. Think about all the emotions we experience.

SADNESS

HAPPINESS

JEALOUSY

ANGER

SHAME

JOY

BOREDOM

SURPRISED

CURIOSITY

AND SO MANY MORE...

If you're human you will experience a lot of different emotions!

Emotions can be helpful. They can motivate and fuel us to finish jobs and accomplish goals, to be more aware of our actions and reactions, and also to ignite empathy for others. However, you must know this one big juicy fact:

Your emotions are NOT in charge!

They are not the boss; just as we've learnt that thoughts aren't either! They are just part of an alert system to check in.

And here's juicy fact #2.

Image Attribution: www.freepik.com/free-photos-vectors/cartoon
Cartoon vector created by pch.vector — www.freepik.com.

YOU get a say in what happens. You get to choose.

Yes you do. Emotions aren't supposed to be the captain of the ship and sail you around whatever sea they want to travel on. They are more like the waves that are supposed to come and go the same way that thoughts do.

And here's the great news...when we allow them to come and go without giving them much response, they will just do their thing without having a huge impact on how we function.

When we can become the observer of our emotions, and choose the response that we have to that emotion, then we can really begin to transform our lives.

Let me say that again.

If you observe your emotions and choose your own response to them, you can transform your life.

Otherwise, the fact is, you'll be at the mercy of your own emotions. They should NOT be running the show. You're the ring master, okay?!

Most of the time though, that's what happens. Without self-awareness and training, our emotions run us all over town. You have to choose the hand you want to play.

"Emotions are within us, no matter how big they feel, they will never be bigger than we are."
— Dr Nat

you Have to CHoose tHe
HaND you waNt to PLay

When we have an emotion, anger for example, we often try to either suppress it (push it away perhaps by drinking alcohol) or we may act on it (yell at the kids, drive erratically, or kick the rubbish bin). We allow how we feel to be in charge of what we do, and then we *become the feeling*. For example, if we feel anger then we become angry, and we behave angrily.

This is when the emotion dominates us (we're at its mercy) rather than us feeling the emotion and then choosing what we need to do in response to that feeling. See the difference?

Sometimes we do not need to do anything with our feelings. Just noticing that we have a particular feeling and observing it, feeling it, naming it, and allowing it to be there — will do the trick. It works wonders when you realise you don't have to manage them like a juggling act at the circus. You can get on with your life and do what you need to do.

Other times emotions may be a sign or an alert that we need to take action or to change something.

Our job is to simply:

1. Notice the feeling
2. Label it
3. Ask yourself: What is this emotion trying to tell me? What is the intention of this emotion? What does it mean? What do I need to do about this, if anything?

This allows us to understand what response is more helpful and what response is unhelpful. The test is not to be taken over by feelings or ruled by them, but to notice them and to know when to do something with that emotion and when not to.

We need to acknowledge that it is just an emotion.

And emotions are within us, so no matter how big they feel, they will never be bigger than we are.

We are the container for the emotions. We still get to choose. If the feeling seems intense, often by noticing it and naming it, the intensity can reduce. It's like dialing down the heat.

The main job of a feeling is to get your attention!

So, when you notice and acknowledge the feeling, your brain knows that you have received the message, and it can then reduce the message (that is, the emotion) it is sending.

If a response or action is required, then we need to consider doing it.

The action could be to:

- have a good cry
- do some journaling
- have that difficult conversation
- leave that relationship
- tell the truth
- spend more time with family and friends
- go for a run

- leave that job or change careers
- have some time to yourself
- keep doing what you're doing.

It could just be to listen and notice. Notice the message and just allow the feeling to come and go. It's just a feeling. It's just energy in motion — *e-motion*.

It's not a direction or an order; it's just a feeling.

We do not need to react or respond to it, but just notice, acknowledge, label it, and then choose an action. Sometimes it may be to get on with what you were doing, finish what you promised, or do what you said you would do. Sometimes it is to take action based on what you are feeling and what you need to do to acknowledge and address that message.

The problem is that there is *no right way* or predetermined way to know what you need to do and when. It is part of learning and understanding yourself and becoming a keen observer of your mind and emotions.

Emotions are an important part of being a human being. They can be great motivators for action and change. However, when left untethered to run riot, they can be very painful and can be intense and ongoing if we choose to try to suppress them. The best thing we can do for emotions is to notice and acknowledge them. Give them a voice — say *'hey, I'm feeling sad right now'* or *'I'm feeling angry right now'*. Just by doing this we can often reduce the intensity. Then ask yourself — how do I need to respond to this emotion right now? Or do I need to respond? Can I just let it come and go, as it does already?

"You are the captain of your ship on the sea of emotion. We cannot control the sea but we can choose how we respond to it and steer our ship in the best direction, working with the sea, not against it."

— Dr Nat

THE PHYSICAL EFFECTS OF YOUR THOUGHTS AND FEELINGS

Many people are surprised when I explain how our thoughts and feelings affect our body; or more accurately our physiology. Your body is an incredible factory for making feelings and physical responses. It works 24/7.

These physical reactions manifest in a way that can be measured against our normal functions. For example, after a very threatening thought such as, *'I can't get through this'* or *'This is too much, I can't handle this'*, a stressful emotion of overwhelm is produced. This will likely trigger the sympathetic nervous system in my body to prepare for the fight-or-flight stress response.

Hormones and chemicals such as adrenaline and cortisol will be released into my body in preparation for the stress response. My heart rate will increase, muscle tension will increase so that I am stronger for running and fighting, and blood flow to my arms and legs will increase for extra oxygen and energy. Blood flow will decrease in areas of my body not considered necessary for running and fighting for survival, this decrease to my digestive system may cause nausea, while the prefrontal cortex of my brain (controlling thinking, planning and logic) will also receive less blood and oxygen, and will reduce my ability to think straight, concentrate, or problem solve. That's a hell of a lot of physical activity just from one emotion called "overwhelm" right?! It's a chaotic circus of activity in there.

Other effects of the stress response include jelly-like legs (because of adrenalin), having to pee a lot, shortness of breath or having difficulty breathing or swallowing, as though I have a lump in my throat. It may also mean that I have difficulty sleeping, especially if I continue to trigger this stress response continually or severely over a period of time, without some effective relaxation. Can you relate to any of these? I'm sure you can.

It's really important to know that this is all *normal* when we feel stressed. Yes, you're perfectly normal.

Yes, it feels like shit. Yes, it sometimes feels like you're going to die. It is designed that way to make you feel like you are about to die so you *get moving* — so that you run or fight for your life. It's our innate survival response; it's meant to feel bad. And it is *good* that it feels bad because it is the response to a physical threat or death; so you need to run or fight. It's rather brilliant don't you think?

The modern problem is that we're triggering this physiological, stress response to non-physical threats like worry, anxiety and tension — and this is highly unhelpful in these situations. This is when we need to stay very calm and relaxed so that we can work out what we need to do. We actually need blood to flow to the brain with oxygen so we can think logically and clearly and problem-solve.

We don't want to trigger the release of adrenaline and cortisol and feel like we are going to die. This is why managing our responses to our thoughts and feelings is so helpful. If we don't trigger this physiological reaction, then we can better manage the event or situation in a calm relaxed state and achieve a better result. Remember the scenario of paramedics walking calmly into an emergency? They are trained to be calm so they can think clearly and problem solve.

If you had a heart attack would you prefer a calm paramedic attend to you or a stressed one frantically searching for the cardiac paddles?

So, what can you do?

We can all help ourselves by managing our physiological state and relieving some of the symptoms through physical movement and exercise. Yes, don't worry I'm not about to load you with another exercise program. But think about exercise in a way to help you reduce stress and reset your balance.

Exercise helps to burn off those pesky stress chemicals— adrenaline and cortisol and it often releases feel-good hormones like endorphins. Yay! Gimme some of those babies. It can also rebalance the oxygen and carbon dioxide levels and release tension in our muscles, which all helps us to feel calmer.

It can be helpful to do diaphragmatic breathing exercises or to have a relaxing massage or bath; all designed to help relax the physical body and activate the parasympathetic nervous system (the opposite of the sympathetic nervous system). This is why people encourage us to do these things when we feel stressed. 'Oh is that why?' I hear you say — absolutely!

You are now armed with a perfect and valid reason as why you should get that massage, take that bath, go to kickboxing class or join yoga.

It is also important to consider what we ingest or don't ingest that can impact our physical bodies. Now don't get me wrong, I'm not selling you any diet fads or promoting any 'lose 10lbs in 3 days' quick fix schemes. I'm talking about overblown things like excessive sugar or caffeine. These can exacerbate a stress-like response in our body. Not drinking enough water is also a factor, so eating healthy, fresh food and drinking plenty of water is a base line that all our bodies need for our nervous systems to function well. You don't have to turn vegan or start a fresh water spring in your backyard, just think *"hey can I drink more water?"* or *"maybe I can cut down those 3 teaspoons of sugar in my coffee."*

Ask yourself what *really* relaxes you and add it into your life as a priority! It could be exercise, sex or even a massage. You can even do all those things at one time. ☺

It could be that you love to bushwalk or bike ride or sit on a hill looking at the sunset. What are those things that make you go mmmmmm?

What makes you feel peaceful?

What helps you reduce stress?

What do you need to feel more balanced?

REAL TALK FOR REAL CHANGE

- Emotions are part of our internal system that communicates different messages to us. If you're human (which I believe you are) you will experience a lot of different emotions!
- Your emotions are not the boss of you. You are the boss of them. You have a choice as to how you respond to it.
- If you observe your emotions and choose your own response to them, you can transform your life.
- Help your body handle all the myriad of emotions by exercising, breathing well and releasing feel-good hormones.

CHAPTER 10

DON'T JUST SIT THERE — ACT!

So, now that you know why we do what we do…it's crunch time. Here is the whole game: **taking better actions.**

Yep, it's not all knowledge and know-how. You have to get up off your bum and make some moves! It's all good and well to make plans, visualise, have a success chart, but nothing works until you do something with them.

What we change (or don't change) is at the heart of this journey. It is this step that really makes the difference. Why? Because without taking action and actually changing our unhelpful actions — our life stays the same. **Nothing changes without action.** Action determines the results we get (or don't get) and the success we have (or don't have).

The reason for all of these powerful methods is to help us take action and make changes — this is the entire game. The big game called *changing your life.*

When we have a new understanding or have learnt something for the first time, and we actually use it to change something — then we have found the key. **Actually *using* what we know, is the part that will make the biggest difference.** As Albert Einstein said, "Nothing happens until something moves."

Personally, I like to really understand something before I can get on board for making a change. It's not the only thing I need to make changes, however it is an important first step for me.

For example it was important for me to understand the fight-or-flight response so I could then understand the rationale for doing the 4-7-8 breathing technique. Otherwise, I can tell you I wasn't going to just sit around and count my breaths — I have to know why! Once a concept makes good sense to me, I can run with it. Prior to that — nup! No chance. But once I understand it and really know why — then okay, I'm on board and say let's go (mostly!).

That's also why, when I meet a person for their first session I like to begin with an explanation of the instincts governing human behavior, to explain the reason why these exercises help calm our nervous system and its reactions. Why they make practical sense. I'm not going to tell someone to sit around and count their breaths just for the sake of it. I have to know it WILL change their physiology.

So, let's get this show on the road. Let's review our 'actions' by dividing them into two obvious types:
Helpful (adaptive)
Unhelpful actions (maladaptive).

Many of the behaviours that are triggered by the stress response can be considered *unhelpful* in our modern-day life.

Things like yelling, aggression or flight responses like avoidance, numbing out. Or the more excessive behaviours, like taking drugs, sleeping pills or alcohol. These are often behaviours that stem from our nervous systems being triggered by an event and going into an acute stress response.

Unfortunately, while these unhelpful behaviours feel good in the moment, they only give us temporary relief. They only scratch the itch of the stress response, temporarily relieving the stress of the urge to fight or run.

When we take unhelpful actions, everything in our life gets tangled up in a big mess.

Our stress response gets relieved temporarily (perhaps by drinking too much alcohol), then we feel shit again, and so often we repeat the same shitty behaviour again. What's more, that shitty behaviour that we started with often goes on to create way more problems than the original event that occurred and the original feeling of just being stressed about a single thing. The unhelpful actions can often create layers on top of the original issue. What a mess. You'll even hear people say, "Oh, my life is a mess" or "I'm in such a mess."

Often I see people caught up in these vicious cycles.

- The unhelpful action starts out as a way to manage stress, but then this action compounds the original problem or issue.
- The behaviour begins as a way of feeling better or relieving the stressful feelings or thoughts, and then our unhelpful action turns into a stressor itself, thus creating more stress, worse feelings, and more problems in life.

We are then caught in a vicious cycle: finding temporary relief from the stress by continuing our unhelpful actions which creates more stress and fuels the need for more relief! We've created a trap for ourselves and so we despair our life will always be this way! Arghhhhh!!!!

BREAKING THE CYCLE

How do we break the cycle? How do we bust our beliefs, for example, the misconception that guilt is helpful to be a better person? How do we stop unhelpful actions that create more stress?

Next time you reflect on something you've done that you may regret, instead of self-reproach, I want you to acknowledge what has happened, acknowledge what you have done and **take responsibility** for it.

In my experience, there is a tendency in our society to think that if we don't feel bad and beat ourselves up over something we've done, then we mustn't care enough or we're bad people. As though; 'the worse I feel, the better person I am' — I'm here to say — what a load of hog shit! By now, I hope we recognise the downward spiral of negative thoughts; 'the worse I feel about myself, the worse actions I take'. We all know this — right? So why do we do it? Bloody human nature!

Now — this is not blame, this is *responsibility* — that is, you have the ability to understand some of the reasons for your behaviour and then *respond* — cool huh?! Then you can work out what went wrong and figure out how to change your response and behave differently next time. That's it! Nothing more dramatic required. Taking responsibility is saying 'I have the ability to respond'. This can be very empowering. Of course, to do that we need to be in a calm, relaxed state because we need to problem-solve.

The best way to solve a problem is with a calm, open mind. (We have been through it but I think it's worth another special mention.)

To do this we need to:

1. Understand what is happening
2. Understand why it is happening
3. Train ourselves to use the strategies that make a difference.

Sound good? It is. It's a simple three step dance.

Just like an unhealthy person can train themselves to get fit, we can train unhealthy beliefs to become more helpful and adaptive ones.

Reducing stress minimises our body's stress response and helps us understand and observe our thoughts differently. We can choose our response and manage our feelings in a different way. We then take more helpful actions and untangle our mess. Voilà!

So first you need to find a way to chillax.

The following ideas are real examples that my clients and I have used to help find a calm, relaxed state in order to problem-solve.

HELPFUL ACTIONS

Diaphragmatic breathing ... exercise ... mindfulness ... having a relaxing bath ... journaling ... catching up with a supportive friend ... volunteering at a shelter ... slowing down our actions ... scheduling our time in blocks and keeping our number of focuses limited ... starting a garden ... colouring ... having that difficult conversation ... petting a dog ... hugging someone ... cooking a yummy dish ... doing a crossword ... learning a new skill ... cleaning out a cupboard ... getting more organised ... putting a new system for managing mail and bills in place ... sharing the pick-up and drop-offs with another parent ... swapping baby-sitting time with someone so you can have a date ... listening to your favourite songs ... meditating ... yoga ... joining a bushwalking group ... learning how to knit ... watching some inspirational TED talks ... YouTubing funny things that make you laugh out loud ... finding an old favourite book and rereading it or listening to it on audio ... reading a new book ... becoming fascinated with something new ... learning a new language or sign language ... helping out at a school or ...

What are some stress-less strategies or activities you could use?

....

....

....

....

....

....

....

....

....

....

....

....

BASE ACTIONS ON YOUR VALUES

One of the best guides that I use for working out what actions to take is based on what I truly value. So rather than there being right and wrong actions, I look at what is most helpful first and then consider what is most important to me. I base many of my decisions around my values. Why? Because then I live my values. And living your values sets you up for a good, congruent, meaningful life.

WHAT ARE VALUES?

Values are things that you believe are important to you, as the word suggests, *things you value*. They are often defined as the principles or standards of one's behaviour; one's judgement of what is important in life. Now this is different for everyone. I might value education and learning (which I do) and my neighbor may value financial success. This doesn't mean either one of us is wrong, it just means what I value is mine and what he values is his.

Now, here's the thing: **we can more easily take action on things that we value.**

As one of my important values is continual education and learning, I may consider taking a new course (action) because it feels good when I am doing it, and it will move my life forward in an area that is important to me. So an action I could take might be to read a book on a new therapy.

If I also consider optimum health as an important value, then I might choose something that forwards this value at the same time. So I could learn how to play baseball (and then education and health-based values are fulfilled here). Or maybe I can teach kids some breathing and mindfulness techniques (also being health and education-based), while also forwarding my own mindfulness practice and increasing my ability to better manage my stress levels. Tick, tick, tick! I also have a value on having fun, so these actions would also be fun for me and likely to be helpful in reducing and better managing my stress levels.

If you head toward your values, the actions come to you more easily. They're fun and simple.

As we are all different, different actions will work for different people.

For example, I find watching a bit of TV at night very relaxing and it puts me into a good relaxed mode for sleep (provided what I'm watching is fairly low-key). While music for me is very stimulating as it's my alarm clock and what I listen to when getting ready in the morning. But I know that for some people it can be the opposite. So we all need to find what works for us best to achieve the result we are looking for. There is no one-size-fits-all approach, although I always suggest that people try some new or different ideas, as sometimes you just never know if you'll find something fulfilling or helpful until you try it.

Some people cook, some people binge watch Netflix, some people garden. Do what floats your boat. My motto has always been 'do what works as long it doesn't hurt you or anyone else'.

IDENTIFY YOUR VALUES

1. What do you value most in life? List what's most important to you — do it fast starting with most important, and then next most important, and so on. Keep going until you get to around 20 values. Be specific.
2. What do you value in relationships?
3. What do you value in your career or work?
4. What inner traits do you value the most?
5. What do you value in terms of health/wellbeing?

ASK THE WHY QUESTION

Once you have made a list of your values, then ask yourself *why*. For example, why is being a great role model and parent important to you? Clarifying your purpose (or your why).

WRITE UP YOUR MANTRA

Write up a personal mantra about your values and why these are important to you. Read this daily.

For example:

Value Mantra: I am a great role model and parent to my children.

Why: This is because it is important to me that they grow into strong, happy healthy human beings.

Value Mantra: I love learning and always look for opportunities to grow and educate myself further.

Why: This is so that I can continue to provide the best possible tools and techniques for myself and my clients to live the best life possible.

Value Mantra: I communicate my needs to my partner and take time out for myself on a regular basis.

Why: This is because I am no good to anyone if I am depleted and grumpy.

Value Mantra: I am passionate in my work, always focused on contributing and making a difference in people's lives, each and every day.

Why: This is because I get joy and energy from seeing others thrive.

Value Mantra: I take care of myself by exercising regularly, checking in on my emotional self, and eating fresh, healthy food.

Why: This is so that I have an abundance of energy for myself, my family/friends, my clients, and in whatever I choose to do.

> *"My motto is — do what works as long it doesn't hurt you or anyone else."*
>
> *— Dr Nat*

MAKE YOURSELF A VALUES BOARD

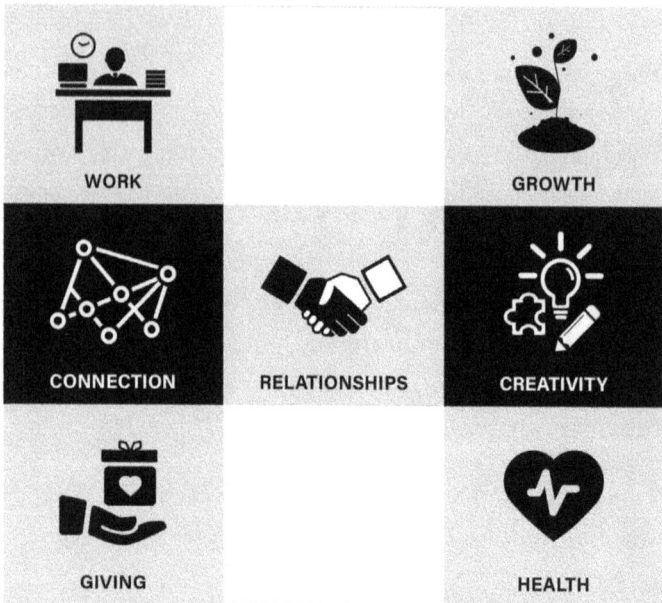

WORK		GROWTH
CONNECTION	RELATIONSHIPS	CREATIVITY
GIVING		HEALTH

You can also use your mantras in a visual display by making a Values Board. Place all your Value Mantras on a board and use photos and pictures that make you feel connected and congruent with your mantras. You can also list your whys below each photo and create a truly unique collage.

VALUES-BASED ACTIONS

The next step is to take some actions to fulfill those values. It's all about taking values-based actions. So if my value is being healthy so that I have lots of energy, then I may stop drinking so much alcohol, and go for a walk instead. That would be a values-based action.

Ask yourself now:

What actions could I take right now to fulfil my values and move my life forward? List three.

Action 1

....

....

Action 2

....

....

Action 3

....

....

Will these actions I am about to take, serve me and create the kind of life I want? If so, how?

....

....

....

....

....

....

....

....

....

....

CHAPTER 11

SELF-CARE — IT'S YOUR JOB

ALL TOGETHER NOW

Let's revisit the cycle we've been unravelling so far. It's important to remember that making a change at *any point* in the cycle will help to break the pattern and reduce these interchangeable triggers or more specifically change the *way* that you manage them. So — good news!

The bad news is…no-one can do this for you! The job is YOURS! Yes, just like the old adage, "If it's meant to be it's up to me."

DR. NAT'S COGNITIVE BEHAVIOURAL THERAPY CYCLE

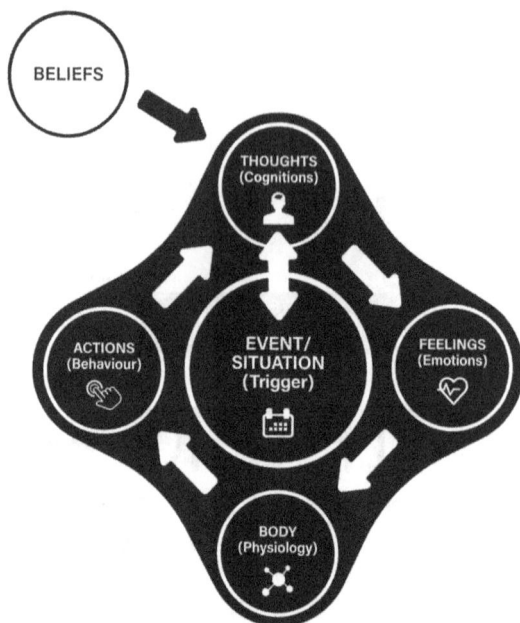

So the best way to take care of yourself and make a change is to break your own negative cycle.

The best strategy to break your cycle is to make a change near the start of the cycle.

This gives the quickest way to stop the pattern and create a lasting impact. For example, if we made a change in our physiology and started taking some natural or pharmaceutical medication for anxiety to change our chemicals or hormones, that could help initially for sure. However, if we still keep the same patterns of unhelpful thinking, then medication or supplements are unlikely to help long-term, as we will continue to trigger off the stress response with those same old thoughts.

So while it is fantastic and recommended to make changes in all areas of the cycle for the best result, what can be most helpful is to address the cause.

For example, if I want to improve my health and wellbeing (a value), I would want to stop eating junk food (the current action/behaviour) and eat fresh food instead (a values based action and behaviour).

For the most lasting results I would make a change in my beliefs. I would change beliefs such as "I'm useless", or "I can't do it", or "It's too hard", or "I don't deserve to feel good". By changing these beliefs to something more aligned like, "I am capable and worthy of doing this," would alter the types of thoughts that I have (e.g. "You've got this", "Pick the orange instead of the cake, you deserve to feel good long term"). This would then change my emotional response (e.g. I feel happier, more excited, more hopeful), which would then impact positively on my physiology (e.g. more energy, improved mood). And this would then impact on what I do (e.g. eat fresh food, go for a walk).

By changing what I do, I then reinforce my new belief — which positively impacts my thinking — my emotions — my body — my actions — and around and around we go. Ta-dah!

Having said that, making a change *in any and all areas* of the cycle, will help to make and strengthen the change.

START AT THE START

Go to the beginning of the cycle and consider what creates your stressful response. Generally, it's our beliefs and thoughts because it is these that have us feeling under threat and sends us into a stress response. When we can better observe and understand the thoughts and beliefs that we have, we can then better manage the feelings that are created, which then leads to better actions. *A*-mazing — I know!

Also be aware that this cycle doesn't just flow one way or in one direction — each and every part can start or trigger the other parts.

Thoughts, Feelings, Physiology and Actions can all interact and impact each other. They are tightly woven together.

> *"Making a change in any and all parts of the cycle will strengthen your personal transformation."*
> **— Dr Nat**

BREAKING THE VICIOUS CYCLE

1. Changing My Physiology

Find ways to shift my body from being in a stress response to being chillaxed, using physiological techniques like diaphragmatic breathing and exercise.

2. Changing My Thoughts

Shift from unhelpful thinking or self-talk to more realistic, helpful thinking by examining and considering all of the evidence.

3. Changing My Feelings

Notice and identify how I am feeling — what is the emotion? *(acknowledge, name, observe).*

What do I need to do? Have a good cry, journaling etc?

Choose how you respond to the emotion for the best outcome.

4. Changing My Behaviour

Take actions that are based on what is most important to me — my values. My actions will be influenced by my new way of thinking and feeling.

SELF-CARE IS YOUR JOB

When I first started on my personal development journey as a young 20-year-old, I remember having a timely epiphany: that it was no-one else's job to look after me, but me — it was my job!' At first this rattled me. From the innocence of youth I'd always had in my mind that other people would care for me. Not in a narcissistic way, but simply because that's what had always happened, and I had never considered another viewpoint before.

I had always tried to think about others and do the right thing by them, look after them, and not burden them (my early definitions about caring for someone). So in my naivety of youth, I had assumed this is what others were doing for me, too. Of course that meant when someone didn't look out for me, or did something that I considered uncaring, I was always very shocked and hurt. Until finally, I realised — it wasn't their job to do that — it was mine. I had to be the one to set boundaries in all aspects of my life, to say no when I needed to in order to self-care. Of course it was my job; it made sense.

No one can know you any better than you know yourself. Even if you feel you might not know yourself very well yet, you will still always know more than someone else. No one else can think your thoughts, feel your feelings, know your past experiences, act on your values or know your limits the way that you do.

You are the best person to know what you need and want, even if it's buried deep down.

Sometimes this awareness starts by knowing what you don't want, which is okay too.

What we need and want can change at any given moment too. Other people can never really know this, so how can they be the ones to decide? You must know what's right for you, right now. For example, sometimes you might feel okay to push through and work an extra couple of hours at work each night for a while. At other times, you might not be feeling up to it or have other things you need to do and can't do it. Only you will know at any given time, what you want or need.

SETTING BOUNDARIES

Learning about your needs is essential for self-care and knowing when to say yes and when to say no. Setting boundaries is part of self-care; it allows us to know what's okay and what's not at any given time and it's okay if our needs change. We must be clear with people and not presume they will know our needs; that you might be unwell, too busy or just plain don't want to (which is also okay, by the way).

Knowing your limits, what works for you and under what circumstances is so important. The best part is that you get to decide because it's about you and *for you*. You don't 'have' to do anything. Remember — the only thing you *have* to do is die! Everything else (pretty much) is a choice. Yes there are consequences, but it's still a choice. Your boss won't know that you need a break or that you promised little Susie at home that you'd help her with her homework or watch her ride her bike. You need to be clear and say what works for you and what doesn't work for you.

Most decent, logical people really understand and respect this. Remember, you don't need to explain why — just that you can't, for example, 'I would love to help out, however this doesn't work for me at the moment.' This statement is great because there is nowhere to go and no excuses for people to try to overcome to get you to do it. It's a bit tough at the beginning, and the people-pleaser really wants to justify and give reasons — but overall that doesn't help. Just remind yourself you're doing an important job that only you can do; self-care!

If you decide to say yes to someone's request, they will most likely presume that you have considered the question carefully and that it's truly okay for you to agree to do it. It is not their fault if you needed to (or should have) said no. They will presume that you know your limits. By saying yes to please people, when a polite no was needed, we can feel resentful about the situation, as well as towards the person who asked us. Which, if we think about it, is really unfair. How can they know if you haven't told them? (Remember, none of us are mind readers). **It is *not their job* to assess or know whether you can manage the extra task or favour.** It's *your* job!

Imagine how annoyed and pissed off we would be if someone started assessing our limits for us! God forbid. *'Oh Fred, I was going to ask you to stay back and work, but I know you've stayed the last three nights, so I won't ask you, you're probably tired, and it might be too much for you.'*

How to make me grumpy in less than three seconds flat? Tell me how I feel and then make a decision for me without actually asking me!

The person asking just can't win. We are responsible for our own self-care, setting boundaries and making choices that work for us. Other people can't know these things — it's mission impossible and it's unfair to expect them to know. But somewhere deep down we often expect people to think about us and be considerate. But you have to think about yourself and consider yourself.

The other maddening response is when people worry that you're just trying to please them, they're probably people pleasers themselves and not good at self-care or setting boundaries. They double-check and triple-check your answer; *'Are you sure? Really? You seem tired. What about your (thingy)?'*

So bloody annoying! If I say yes, I own it. Even if a little voice wishes I had said no later, I completely own it, embrace it even. So there is clarity and no resentment or blame experienced by anyone. I am as clear and strong as I can be in my answers. Go girl!

Sometimes you might need to ask for more time to consider a request. I never used to do that, and it created more problems at times. So now I have learnt the benefit of saying, *'Thanks for the opportunity. I will need some time to consider your request, and I will get back to you on Friday.'*

Then I do just that.

DIARISE YOURSELF

As a way of helping me to make better decisions and ensure I am not over-doing it, I have implemented a diary for my life. A diary system is great for everyone, not just for work schedules. A diary helps me to check how balanced or unbalanced my schedule is and what's possible. My desire to embrace all opportunities and say yes quite often, has given me great returns, but it also means my self-care risks getting lost. A diary makes it easy to see in black and white when some time-out is due after a long work period and where self-care has been overlooked. Diaries or calendars are amazing for helping to ensure that we can say yes or no to things powerfully and clearly, and ensuring that we are living in a way that our most important values get a guernsey.

It's important to schedule yourself into your own diary. Where is there time for you?

So here's the bottom line:

1. Work out what makes you feel good and happy.
2. Work out what you need and when you need it.
3. Own it. It's your job, no-one else's. No one else is qualified or can possibly do it. It must be you. It doesn't work to put anyone else in charge of this important need; it changes frequently and in different ways, depending on all your individual experiences moment to moment.
4. Understand that self-care also gives you confidence and empathy when asking for help from others.
5. Schedule time for you (you must take action).

SELF-CARE CRUNCH TIME

Ask yourself these questions:

What do I love doing that I can get lost in?

....

....

....

....

....

....

....

....

What lights me up?

....

....

....

....

....

....

....

....

....

What fills my bucket?

What actions work for me. What actions don't work?

SELF-CARE ACTION TIME

Make some self-care rules. Make your own rules (remember you can do this now).

Here are some examples to get you thinking.

- I have a date with myself every fortnight
- I don't work past 5.30pm
- I don't check work emails once I'm home or logged off
- I leave Saturday morning for walking the dog with my partner
- I don't take on President of the Mothers' Club this year
- I say 'no' to over-time when I'm exhausted.

1. Put this in your diary
2. Relate to them as if *you* are just as important as anyone else in your diary. Actually no, make yourself the MOST important person in your diary. Remember — it's your job to do that! It's time to say, "hell-yeah to self-care."

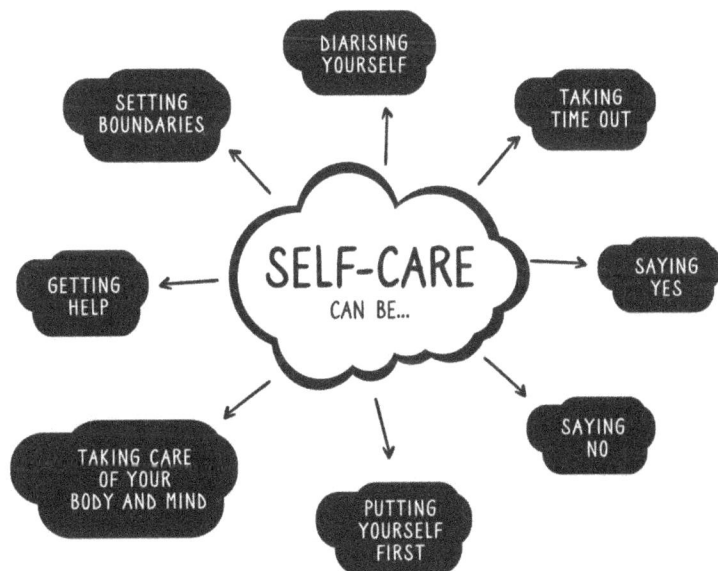

SELF-CARE CAN BE...

- DIARISING YOURSELF
- SETTING BOUNDARIES
- TAKING TIME OUT
- GETTING HELP
- SAYING YES
- SAYING NO
- TAKING CARE OF YOUR BODY AND MIND
- PUTTING YOURSELF FIRST

*"If you don't like something change it.
If you can't change it, change your attitude."*[2]
— Maya Angelou

DR NAT'S
SELF-HELP TOOLS
FOR GREATER LIVING

I'd like to finish this book with some additional self-help tools and thoughts. As I have said before, I only share what I've personally experienced and have seen work in my clinic. Here are some over-arching universal tools for life that have guided me and many of my clients through the rollercoaster ride that we call life. In my opinion, these tools give you a better quality of life and help you unlock your own freedom. I have narrowed these down to my top #7 self-help tools.

#1 REAL ACCEPTANCE — THE KEY TO MOVING ON

Learning about emotional acceptance provides a way forward that ends suffering. The word 'acceptance' gets tossed around quite a bit nowadays and like any word it is open to interpretation. In my work I hear people say, "I must be more accepting," or, "If only I could accept what is going on."

For many people, they assume this means they want to be *okay* with what's happened. They want to be able to shrug and let it go without looking back, basically brushing it under the carpet. In my experience this is the opposite of a helpful, healthy interpretation of real acceptance.

Acceptance is finding the willingness to acknowledge something in our lives, no matter how much we wish it to be otherwise. It could be that something hurtful or disappointing has happened that we feel strongly affected by; perhaps it's that someone we know just *is* a certain annoying way; or perhaps that we ourselves are a certain stubborn way that we wish we weren't!

Acceptance doesn't mean that we have to like it or want it. Accepting what we like and want is an automatic process; when we *don't* like what something means for us, we have to switch that internal process to *manual*, a much harder task! It's one of the biggest challenges we will face for as long those beeps keep moving up and down on our life's monitor.

A well-known example of the power of acceptance is the courage an alcoholic needs to finally go along to an AA meeting and say the words; 'I am an alcoholic'. From denying and hiding their problems in the dark, this person has brought it out into the light and accepts they have a problem with alcohol.

Personally I don't agree with reinforcing the concept, 'I am an alcoholic' over and over, but to say 'I have a problem' is certainly the first step to change. After all, as the saying goes, you can't change what you don't acknowledge.

Acceptance Gives Us Something Unique

Acceptance is not about giving up on a situation by saying, *oh well, that's just the way it is.* This might give us a little break from the pressure but no peace will ever come from quitting; in fact, cynicism often grows in its place.

The first benefit from true acceptance is a level of relief; it allows us to drop the struggle, stop fighting it, and stop resisting it. What we resist persists. I know how bloody hard it is to keep resisting the reality of a situation, of holding on too tight. It takes endless energy and effort, which can be so debilitating. I have seen too many people turn to drugs (medicinal or recreational) as a way of denying or numbing out to cope with the issue.

I resisted the futility of my first marriage for many years. Early on, I began to suspect (and deny) that we were not right for each other. We were such different people with very different backgrounds, values, parenting styles, work ethics, moral compasses etc. I was turning 30 though so I was determined to make it work even if it killed me. I completely resisted the idea that he was not the one.

I spent around ten years of my life resisting this reality and a deep well of confusion, upset, stress, pain, money, and time was exhausted on something that just wasn't right. The moment I finally got it and I said to myself, *'Okay, we just aren't the right fit — like the wrong key to a lock – we just don't fit together,'* I let out years of tension in one enormous breath and accepted it at last. Once I accepted that we didn't fit together, I could start to change things, and eventually I was able to create something new (and it wasn't with him). I am now happily married to a gorgeous man, and I am excited to say that we fit together beautifully, and have done for over ten years now. Yay!

When we finally stop and accept the grief, the anger, the alcoholism, the deceit and the difficult events, we feel a sense of overwhelming relief that we no longer have to fight and resist it.

And then there can be an 'oh shit' moment shortly afterwards. This means that we are likely to experience some feelings when we do accept this something, and part of the acceptance process is accepting these feelings, too. It is the willingness to acknowledge something, and usually it's something we don't like.

Acceptance Leads To Action

What often comes next is an ability to take action; no positive change can be made until after that moment of acceptance. Up until then, there is nothing that can be done because in my world if I don't accept it, the problem (and therefore the solution) does not exist.

Of course you don't have to change it; acceptance is not about whether you take action or not. After you first acknowledge and then accept the situation, you have the power and choice to take action if desired or possible or even if required. But you don't have to do anything you don't want to do (except die at some stage), and the alternative might be that you embrace it and fall in love with exactly how it is; if you've made it work for you, that's great — it's your choice!

Here's an example. Let's say that I don't accept that it's going to get dark tonight. I just don't. I don't like it, I don't want it, and I'm resisting it like crazy. I do not accept that it is going to be dark tonight. In my resistance, I am using a lot of energy *not* to acknowledge the darkness. Of course, in my resistance, I am causing myself some distress and upset and using quite a bit of energy. And, as we all know, regardless of what I don't acknowledge, it is the way it is, and it will get dark. Then where am I left? Sitting in the dark, being miserable most likely.

Alternatively, I could accept that it will get dark tonight. I don't have to like it or want it, but I accept that it will get dark. Of course, in the moment I accept it, I can choose to either embrace it or I can do something about it. What could I do, now that I accept it will be dark tonight? Well maybe, just maybe, I could embrace the darkness, really focus on what there is to love about it and all the benefits of it being dark. Alternatively, I could also just switch on the light.

The deepest level of peace comes from accepting those moments and situations that we have no control over. It can be small moments such as when our partner doesn't pick up the bathmat after a shower, or when a friend is always 30 minutes late to your coffee catch up. In reality, we have no control. We may have some influence (although how many times do we really want to bring it up with them?) but we have no control over their actions (or the rules in their head).

These are things we can continue to resist and fight (which equals stress!) or we can accept them. And the good news is we then have a choice about how we respond or take action. We can accept and embrace this quirk as being part of who they are. Or we can alter our own behaviours to make this work for us — for example, tell our friend the coffee catch-up time is 30 minutes earlier than we plan to be there or use that extra time to read a favourite book or do some emails and social media. Or we can weigh up the positive and negative aspects of any relationship and simply choose not to be around those people.

> *"Nothing will work unless you do."*[4]
> — *Maya Angelou*

So from my own suffering, I have welcomed the lesson of acceptance into my life. I now choose to embrace what it is in all its messiness (it gets easier); or I choose to change those things I have control over (needs a dash or two of courage), or I choose to alter my behaviour so that it works for me (so powerful!). Internally it's about changing your mindset while externally, it's choosing what action to take or not.

Acceptance reduces our struggle and suffering and gives us a new path forward. Now — who doesn't want that?

REAL TALK

- How can you start to accept things that you don't like about yourself or someone else that you have no control over?
- What would you need to do to first accept and then change the things you do have some control over?
- What is not accepting something or someone costing you?
- If you feel resistant, can you at least trial acceptance and see how it feels?

#2 THE GOOD, THE BAD AND THE UGLY INTENTIONS

Every time we communicate, there is an intention.

What is an intention?

The dictionary refers to an intention as:

a) something one intends to do or bring about.

b) 1: the object for which a prayer, mass, or pious act is offered.

2: a determination to act in a certain way: resolve.

Sometimes (mostly) we have good intentions. Yet often we become consumed with getting our own intention across. But it's also an important concept to consider the other person's intention when communicating. I often ask myself this question: What is the intention behind that person's words? What are they trying to convey?

Sometimes people mean to say something with a good intention, they mean well, but it comes out all strange and twisted.

A great example of this is around grief and loss. This is a time where people can say the dumbest things in an attempt to connect or relate to your experience. Grief is a tricky area, an area or emotion that I think is its own magnificent and most painful beast, something that is in a whole different ballpark than most of our other emotions. We are often very awkward and clumsy around grief, so it's a good one to break down what people's intentions are.

One day, after giving birth to my twin stillborn boys at 23 weeks' gestation, a friend saw me for the first time since the boys had died, and I could see he was genuinely confronted and uneasy. *Understandable*, I thought to myself. Anyhow, I know this person to be a kind and loving person who would want nothing more than for me to stop hurting and be okay.

In an attempt to connect with me he said the dumbest thing. He said, 'I know how you feel; when my dad's dog died a few years ago, it was the worst.'

Now, in no way do I want to pretend that I understand what that was like for him, or the depth of his grief. I know and understand that dogs can be everything for some people, and it can be a huge loss. It is often more about what that person or animal meant to us than what or who it was. I get that completely. However, I have to say I was a little taken aback to have the death and loss of my two babies be compared to his dad's dog.

Having experienced this myself, and having talked to other people who have felt outraged at what some people label as other people's insensitivities, I could understand that this may be a little hard to swallow. But, knowing that he would never have meant me any harm or to further upset me, and in fact was more likely to be trying to connect and relate on some level, I took it in my stride. I asked myself: so what was his intention here? Was his intention to make me feel bad or worse, or to try to connect and show empathy and love? In the moment that I understood that his intention was not to make me feel bad but in fact to try and connect with me, I could love him back.

Investigating Intentions Gives You Opportunities

I believe that understanding or knowing someone's intention is a very powerful way of experiencing more love and connection. If we can look at a situation, and know that person, and what their likely intention is going to be, versus what they actually say or do, then we can improve our communication and relationships exponentially. It gives you an opportunity to see beyond the behavior or poor selection of words.

Think about it for a moment. Imagine that you are married to a loving partner and you know that they just want the best for you and for you to be happy and shine. This particular time you are out at a family event and discussing the week. Your partner mentions to the family that they have done all of the cooking and cleaning that week as you have had such a busy week and been away.

Now there are a few ways it could go here, and depending on my view of their intention, it could end well or it could end very poorly. So I ask myself — is their intention to make me feel bad and guilty for not 'putting in'? Is their intention to big-note themselves so they are seen as the martyr and that I'm the lazy sod? Or is it purely to express that we are both busy and both need some love and rest?

Or is it to let the family know that the only reason they have done the majority of the cooking and cleaning is because of how hard I have been working and that I am hardworking and deserve a break after being away?

Knowing my partner and what their intention is likely to be helps me to put into perspective a more helpful and loving response. And if it's not that, it at least helps me to stop and think about it first, and helps me to view it from a few different angles, before I just jump to conclusions and blow my stack at them. I can pause enough to be able to ask a question or two to confirm what their actual intention in the comment was.

Sometimes though I don't want or need to ask — I just don't. This is because I actually don't want to know. I am either very happy to believe that the person meant well or had good intentions, even if they may possibly have not. And really, the bottom line is that, even if I ask, and their intention was evil, what's the chance that they will say that?

So sometimes (not always) I will not check-in for what that person meant by what they said. I will not challenge or get my back up — what for? What will it achieve? How helpful will it be? These are all the questions I ask myself when coming up against this. If I do believe that it will make a difference in the relationship, and/or that person is important to me and plays a larger role in my life, then yes, again sometimes, I will open this up for a discussion.

A discussion — yes, not a brawl, but an opportunity to clarify because, the older I get, the more I realise how wrong I can be. The more I realise that I can't read people's minds, that I often don't know what they're thinking or what they mean by what they've said or their intention. However, if I take a moment and remember who that person is for me, then this can make all the difference to not only how I feel about what they've said but also to how I feel about them, and to the ongoing love and connection that we have together.

REAL TALK

- Before you jump to conclusions, take some time to reflect and ask yourself — what were their intentions?
- You can also use it as a way to check-in with yourself. What are my true motivations and intentions for this situation or person?
- What outcome do I want in this situation, with this person, at this time?
- Who is this person for me (most of the time)? E.g. a loving, kind, well-meaning person or mean spirited?
- Take a moment to consider different perspectives (even if you think you know because you've been shining that crystal ball) — and then choose.

#3 RESPONSIBILITY VS FAULT OR BLAME

"It was me". Why does saying this not feel so good? Why can taking responsibility — or being responsible be so hard for some people? It feels like such a bad idea to be responsible, doesn't it?

And yet, by taking responsibility, it actually means that we can have a say in something. We have the opportunity to change something and not be at the mercy of something or someone else.

So why does being responsible feel so bad? I think it's probably because we confuse the idea of responsibility with the idea of fault or blame. We take it to mean, *'It's my fault, I'm to blame, I'm the bad one or I'm the idiot who did it.'*

It's not a good feeling, and often when we are at fault or being blamed, then this can lead to shitty consequences. *'I have to pay for the car accident repairs; I have to clean up the mess in the kitchen; I have to put up with hearing about how terrible I am and what a bad thing I did for the next two months'*. I get it — why would you want to be at fault or to blame, right?

And although there can even be some good things about admitting fault or being blamed (*what?* I hear you say?), right now I'd just like to focus on what's great about taking responsibility.

What if being responsible meant, being **'able to respond'**, that is 'response-ability'. That it was not about blame or fault but just about having the ability to respond. That feels different now doesn't it? It's kind of powerful and makes me feel that I have some control and some say about what happens, both now and also in the future. I get to respond to this thing (because I'm able to), and that makes me feel empowered rather than disempowered. It means that I can do something about this thing.

When I take no responsibility, I have no power — I have no ability to respond. I am therefore the victim of this thing that happened. I have no say and no power to do anything or to change anything. Now that's a shitty place to be in any situation. However, if I can be responsible, then I know that I can change things and make a difference. I am now back in the driver's seat in this situation. Yippeee!

For example, if I have been in a shitty relationship, while it can feel good initially to blame the other person and say they were the arsehole and they did the arsehole things (and that might even be true), it's not always that helpful for you. The blaming often feels good initially but usually this only feels good in the short-term or temporarily.

In the long term though, blaming means that I will continue to feel shit about the relationship and what has happened. I hold onto upset and grudges, and can feel like a victim. However, if I can say that I can take some responsibility for what happened in that relationship (not blame or fault), then I immediately gain some power back. This is because it now feels like I can learn from this, I had some part, and so I can do something differently next time. I know my part in this situation, and I know I can change it so it won't happen again. While I am a victim and blame someone else, the other person has all the power and I can do nothing.

The Power of Response-Ability

Being *response-able* also helps you think about things differently. You can think to yourself:

- How will I respond to this situation?
- What are my options here?
- How will I do this differently?

It makes you stop and brainstorm the ways you can change this or do things differently next time. Whereas if you believe that you're not able to respond, then why would you even entertain this thought or idea? You wouldn't. You would just sit passively and hope that it never happened again or that someone else could maybe do something about it. Because if you feel unable to respond then this = you have no responsibility.

Even if you take responsibility and then do nothing, that can sometimes be better than having no responsibility and being the victim. Again, I am not talking about blame and fault. I am saying that you get to say to yourself, *'Okay, so it was my responsibility that things went that way; I was not just a victim of others or circumstance'*.

When you do this you are immediately back in the driver's seat. And that is always a better place to be for moving forward and helping things go differently next time.

Note: Using this tool is only for situations where it is helpful or relevant to do so. For example, when we are children, we have much less say and power in our circumstances than when we are adults.

Even so, I do want to say that in any case, blaming may not be particularly very helpful. Rather than blaming, a great question can be, "What can I learn from this?" or "What learning will enable me to move forward in life?" or "What positive lesson did this person or situation teach me that I can use for myself in the future?"

To get the most value from this question, the learning should be positive, for the future, and for you. For example, a learning could be something like "I learnt that I am a strong woman, capable of surviving and getting through way more trauma than I ever imagined I could".

Now that's a great learning.

Over Responsibility

Over-responsibility = being responsible for things you have no control or say in.

While there is a potential for not taking responsibility in some things that we could be responsible for (and in doing this we could get our power back), of course, there is also the potential for us to go the other way (and many of us do this too), and to be over-responsible for things.

Over-responsibility is being responsible for things that we have no business being responsible for, or taking too much responsibility for something that we don't need to or shouldn't do. That is, something happens and then we totally make it all about us and that we have to do something about it. When in reality, it is none of our business and it is not our job to do anything about it.

For example, my boss is angry and screaming at me for forgetting to lock the office door at the end of the day. Who is responsible for what in this scenario? Most of us would usually think something like

"It's my fault I made my boss so angry. If I had locked the door she wouldn't be yelling at me right now". Okay, so who out there does this? I bet there are lots of us. Especially all you Mums — am I right? You know that I am. For example, little Johnny doesn't finish his homework for school and he gets detention. Is there anyone who thinks something like, "If only I had reminded him last night, he could have done it and then he wouldn't have detention". Both of these examples are about being overly-responsible for things that you are not responsible for. "What?" I hear you say? Yes it's true. Because guess what?

We are **not** responsible for:

• How someone else is feeling
• How someone else is behaving
• How someone else is thinking.

So in the above examples, I am responsible for not locking the door, but my boss is responsible for her emotions (e.g. anger) and reaction (e.g. yelling). I have no way of controlling how she feels and how she behaves at all. That is completely up to her. Nothing to do with me at all.

What I did might be a trigger for her, but her reaction is all hers. So when her boss pulls her up for acting unprofessionally, it is nothing to do with me, and everything to do with her. She chose how she responded, not me. It is not my responsibility. If I were to take that on, I would be being overly-responsible. When little Johnny gets detention, no matter what I do or don't do, it is his *response-ability* — he has the ability to respond, that is, do his homework — I don't. It is up to him.

It's Not All About You

Why is it important not to be overly-responsible?

Well, when we do this, we significantly increase our own distress and stress, as these are things we do not have control over. Shock, horror, massive look of surprise! I know right? Believe it or not, we have absolutely nothing to do with how someone else feels, behaves or thinks. The way people react and respond is all a result of… themselves. Only we have the power to change our own feelings, thoughts and behaviours. No-one else, no matter what happens, what others say or do. We always have a say in how we respond.

Not only do we disempower ourselves when we try to be responsible for how others behave, think and feel, but we also take away someone else's power to respond (or their response-ability), when we take it on ourselves. For example, if I say to little Johnny, "I'm so sorry you got a detention at school, I should have reminded you about your homework last night, it's my fault" — then how do you think that will impact on you both?

Likely that little Johnny will not be empowered to make a change to help him remember to do his homework next time (like write it in his diary, set an alarm, write a note and stick it on his desk), he'll just assign blame to you, and be left powerless in the situation, waiting for you to remind him next time. Then what happens when you are not there? And as for me, I'm left feeling guilty and stressed, self-blaming, and trying to work out how I can make sure to remind him next time. And then, even if I do all of this, there is still no guarantee that we avoid the situation next time. That is, even if I do remind him, he may not do his homework and he may still get a detention. This sets up a crazy little ongoing cycle for stress and frustration. This is because the response-ability (the ability to respond) is not sitting where it should be — that is with the person who can or needs to make the change (i.e. the one who is responsible). So…. rather than drive ourselves crazy with being responsible for things we cannot control, let's break that very unhelpful pattern and find another way.

Managing Your Overly Responsible Traits

One of the ways that I started to manage this for myself was to first notice that I was doing that. I might catch myself feeling guilty or bad for something and then I would check in and say to myself "Is this my *response-ability*? Can I control how others feel, what they do, or what they're thinking?"

Once I distinguished that it was not my *response-ability* I would say to myself "This is none of my business. It is not my job".

Remember before when we spoke about self-care being your job — great that's something that is your job. But being overly responsible for things that you cannot control, that you have no say in — that is NOT your job! That is called Crazy Town — don't go there! It won't help you and it's likely it won't help the other person (especially in the long term).

So anytime that you feel the urge to take responsibility for something that is none of your business — just STOP IT! Ask yourself — is this within my power or control? Is this any of my business? Is this my job? If the answer is no to any of these questions — then STOP IT!

Remind yourself it is not your responsibility, it is not your job. Then back away slowly (don't make eye contact — eye contact can be a killer for stopping this over-responsibility) and don't look back. Then do something about the things that you can control, the things that you do have a say in, the things that are your responsibility and are your job to do. When you do this, I promise you, freedom awaits!

REAL TALK

- What is my responsibility? What is the other person's responsibility?
- If I take it on as my responsibility (when it is not), how will that negatively impact me? How will it negatively impact the other person?
- To help break the habit — first notice the guilt and/ or feeling bad — check by asking yourself — is this actually my responsibility?
- Remember — you cannot control what others say, how they think, or what they do — it's not your responsibility — it's theirs! You have no ability to respond in this case. You actually can't do it. So don't!
- If it's not your responsibility — say to yourself — "It's not my job, it's none of my business" — you will save yourself bucket loads of stress and frustration.

PS. This is not to say that we can't assist people or encourage them, but this is very different than taking responsibility for something that is none of our business.

#4 WORKABILITY AND HELPFULNESS — RIGHT VS WRONG AND GOOD VS BAD

What if there was no right and wrong? What if there was no good and bad? What! Of course there is a good and bad; of course there is a right and wrong. Really? Who says? How do you know?

If there's one thing I really want to achieve from writing this book, it's to stop people blindly buying into stuff without first questioning it and then powerfully choosing it. We've all done it; I've done it. Never questioning, just accepting that it is a certain way because that's the way it has always been. Well to that I say — so what?

Now, really — who says what is right and what is wrong? Who is it? Oh…society, oh okay. Not! Who is society? Everyone! Really? Everyone? Well no not everyone. Oh okay, then who? Well, some people. Oh okay, so then some people say that. Well, okay that sounds more accurate. Now, how do they know what's right and wrong, good and bad? Can you see where this is heading? That's right — to *nowhere*! Because this is all subjective and usually unquestioned. It's just some opinions of some people (or yourself) that you've bought into and taken on board. You've also taken on the idea that there actually IS a right and wrong, and a good and bad.

So here's something to think about — what if there wasn't right/wrong and good/bad? What if they didn't exist? What if there were just different choices, with each choice having different consequences? And what if sometimes what seemed like the wrong decision at the time, then turned out to be the right one later on? Then what? Was it the right or the wrong way? And how would you know?

'Oh great', I hear you saying, 'So how will I be able to choose? How will I know what to do?'

To illustrate this point, I remember a poignant story told by the great Alan Watts[3]. It was a story about a Chinese farmer whose horse ran away. That evening, all of his neighbours came around to commiserate. They said, "We are so sorry to hear your horse has run away. This is most unfortunate." The farmer said, "Maybe."

The next day the horse came back bringing seven wild horses with it, and in the evening everybody came back and said, "Oh, isn't that lucky. What a great turn of events. You now have eight horses!" The farmer again said, "Maybe."

The following day his son tried to break one of the horses, and while riding it, he was thrown and broke his leg. The neighbours then said, "Oh dear, that's too bad," and the farmer responded, "Maybe."

The next day the conscription officers came around to conscript people into the army, and they rejected his son because he had a broken leg. Again all the neighbours came around and said, "Isn't that great!" Again, he said, "Maybe."

Watts summed up this story by saying, "the whole process of nature is an integrated process of immense complexity, and it's really impossible to tell whether anything that happens in it is good or bad — because you never know what will be the consequence of the misfortune; or, you never know what will be the consequences of good fortune."

Is There Really a Right Way?

There are a couple of things that I use to guide my decision making that do not involve the torturous, body and mind twisting, excruciatingly painful decision-making process of asking oneself, 'Is this the right decision/partner/house/job for me, etc.?'

Here's what I know — there really is no 'right' one. It just doesn't exist. Really! Unless you say it is — then it is the right house/job/partner. But only because you say it is. It is whatever you say it is. If I pick a house, whether or not it's the right house all depends on whether or not I say it's the right house — there is no 'right house' (or decision or whatever!), only what I say it is. Same with wrong and good and bad, all those labels are completely subjective.

So now what? Well, there are a few ways to move forward and make those decisions. One way is to ask yourself, *'Does this work for me?'* If we're thinking about creating *work-ability*, then this is a whole different thing than the good-bad thing. I know there might be some people who think — well, if there's no good or bad, then society will go to the dogs; it will be chaos. But what if we said we have rules and laws, NOT to distinguish people who are good/bad and right/ wrong but because the rules provide *work-ability* in our society. That is, it works for us to stop at a red light, or not to steal from others, or to pay taxes. What if it's not good or bad if you do or don't do it but more that it works for us to do (or not do) these things. It helps us to live in a society in a way that is workable for many people sharing a space and resources.

If we applied this question to trying to choose a house, rather than asking, 'Is this the right house for me?' what if you asked, 'Does this house work for me?' This then might have you start to look at the pros and cons of the house, where it is, the layout, think about what you might be okay with, and things that are not okay for you in a house or living environment. Is it a house that I can make work for me? Same-same for a partner, in a round-about kind of way.

In making some other decisions, like — should I go back to university? Buy a motorbike?

You could also apply the workability question — how would this work for me? You could also ask — how important is this for me to do and why? Another good question is — how helpful would this be?

These kinds of questions all open up the idea, and get you to do some work so that you can make a decision in a way that is more empowering for you. This way it allows for you to consider elements and weigh things up. Ultimately, it is still your decision, and it is still subjective. However it is one that you can own and not be at the mercy of the right-wrong and good-bad Gods. This way you have looked at it in a way that allows you to consider many of the possible consequences and outcomes, and then own it — like a boss! Not like a puppy.

And, in the end, if you just choose whatever, you can own that, too. Knowing that there is no right/wrong or good/bad, just a choice with consequences. It's all about what you say, because it is whatever you say it is — the right one, the wrong one, the good one, the bad one.

The other reason I prefer not to make negative subjective judgements about these things or decisions is because of the way it can leave me feeling. If I am left feeling shit about my choice, then I am less likely to want to make a choice again. I will feel fearful or reticent to choose again, or not trust myself to make a 'good' decision in the future. This leaves me feeling fearful and doubting myself even more.

I get really clear in the moment that whatever I chose at that time, is because I was meant to have that experience so that I could learn more and get to where I am now. Or sometimes it's just that I didn't know what I didn't know, and now I know more, so I can choose differently. I now know more about what works for me and what is most helpful for me. And thinking about it this way is what works for me and what is more helpful for me, so that's what I do. Not because it's the 'right' thing or a 'good' thing to do, just because it's more helpful and it works for me to be able to move forward faster and to live my best life.

"To have change, you have to make a change."
— Dr Nat

REAL TALK

- There is no actual good/bad or right/ wrong — it's just whatever we declare and say that it is.
- Focus on *work-ability* — ask yourself — does this work for me/my family/society? Will this be more helpful?
- Consider the consequences — everything has consequences — even not doing anything or not deciding has consequences.
- Sometimes it can seem like the 'wrong' choice (less desirable) but it works out to be the 'right' choice (more desirable) — and vice versa!

#5 PUSH YOUR BRAVERY BUTTONS

It is one thing to say, 'Here, you should try this,' or 'You should do that' — it's another thing to set off and actually do it yourself. Obviously I truly believe in the help I offer and the information I give to people, but I know it's a whole other story to turn that advice into action and do the hard stuff yourself.

Life often calls for you to step up not just once or twice, but repeatedly. You have to find the strength to keep going, keep getting back up, over and over again throughout your life. It is not easy.

Like many people I've met, I've had to face many harsh realities and put myself out there so many times to overcome huge obstacles in my life. But after these experiences it takes great bravery to *keep* putting yourself out there after a setback. To put yourself on the line again in some way, expose yourself to loss or pain, step up and find confidence, take new risks, be vulnerable to love — to keep walking your path in life is a whole other ballgame.

I always say to people to make sure you continue to put yourself in the shoes of the other person you are working with because we can quickly forget what it's like, how it feels, and what it takes to do things differently and to make changes. It's why when I was a trainer I used to sit in on other people's trainings. Not just so I could learn some stuff, but also so I could remember. So I could remember what it is like to be a participant. How it feels to sit there listening to someone, to have to do tasks, to work with others (especially to do work in groups — I bloody hate working in groups), to answer questions publicly, etc. Or I say to go and be a client with a psychologist or a coach. To go and be exposed to other methods and knowledge, but also to go and remember how and what that feels like. To remember how confronting and difficult it can be to sit across from someone who you are being vulnerable and completely exposed with.

At times it's terrifying, exhausting, and embarrassing — and sometimes it's all of those things all at once — and it's good to remember that. It's actually vital to remember that because remembering helps us to tap back into our compassion and empathy, and to use this to work with someone in a way that is most helpful for them. Also, because I know that when I'm working with say a coach, and they don't really 'get it' or get what it takes for me to do something, then it is way harder for me to feel connected with them and for me to then step out and do the work. If someone really gets it and can have compassion for me, and then really stand for me to do it (knowing the difference that it will make), then I'm all for that.

Give Yourself Permission to Be Human

As a way of getting back into the world after the death of my twin boys (I didn't feel ready to return to work as a psychologist straight away) I decided to return to university and complete a Graduate Diploma in Education to become a primary school teacher. I had the thought that if I couldn't have more children then maybe I was meant to be doing that instead (how wrong we can be!).

Even though I had completed my third university degree only seven years earlier, things at university had changed — a lot! You could talk and eat and drink in the library — what! *And* you had to check your own books and materials out of the library — what! Where was the quiet, shy librarian with the glasses? University had vastly changed in the way that things were done since I had left. The content was still there, but the delivery was incredibly different.

So here I was in my 40s, back at university, having no clue how to navigate this foreign system. Everything was online — everything was submitted, accessed, and shared online, even conversations were online — and this was the 'on-campus' degree! Vulnerability, here we come. It was really stressful trying to work it all out. It was also really hard being back in the starting position again — being older and after having done this a few times before, and to have been recently working as a successful psychologist. On a whole new level, I had to remember what it was like to not know what you were doing, to feel confused and lost, to have to rely on others for help, to be at the starters post again, to be under the influence and control of others in more powerful positions.

The point is though, although very stressful at times (okay, many times) — it was great. It was an awesome reminder that I'm just human. As I often say to my clients, 'I'm just a stupid human bumbling around doing the best I can in this thing we call life. And sometimes I'm not. Sometimes I'm magnificent and knowledgeable, smart and skillful. That's the funny, crazy, amazing thing about being human'.

That just because I might know a lot about one subject, or have a lot of experience or skill in one thing, doesn't mean I am above having a human being experience. Being human is what gives us our connection with others. It's when we share our vulnerability and expose our feelings to others that we truly and deeply connect.

One of the best things I've ever done for myself is to give myself permission to be human. This means that sometimes I will stuff up, get scared, say or do the wrong thing, feel angry or sad, forget important things, or make a big mistake. This is all part of being human. And I'm okay with that now — well *mostly*! Ha! See, there's my humanness showing up again. Too funny!

Being a human requires great bravery; being vulnerable and exposed means we are open to being hurt. But I believe the people who are most vulnerable are the bravest. And because of this, they are the ones who are most rewarded. For they will take the risks and be willing to fail, fall, and be seen to be exposed. However, they are also the ones that we love and connect with the most, and the ones who we want to be with and be around. Being brave requires us to take a chance, a chance that for all that we are and for all that we are not, the risk is worth the reward.

#6 TRUST YOURSELF

So many people run around saying, 'Trust yourself'. But what does that actually mean? And how the hell do you do it? I grew up in a time where authority was everything. The doctors were Gods, our parents were the boss, and teachers knew everything. These were the people I listened to, regardless of my own thoughts, feelings, and knowledge. As I grew, anytime someone was in a position of power, my boss at work, the lecturer at university, I felt that they

195

must know more and be better than me, so I just followed. Doing this meant that I stopped listening to me. I stopped listening and so then that little voice inside of me probably just gave up and stopped talking to me — what was the point — everyone else knew better.

So that little voice inside of me — (not the crap-talking blah-blah one) but the intuitive one that says, 'Maybe that isn't right for me; I think I can do better; I need to be part of something else; this person isn't good for me; I deserve more; I am not happy,' was shut down. It got really quiet and then it just shut down. I stopped listening, it stopped talking, and one day I woke up and didn't know who the hell I was or what the hell I wanted. While people were saying — Well, what does your heart say? What do you like? What makes you happy? If you could do anything, what would you do? — it made not a pinch of difference because I had no voice talking to me anymore, there was nothing being said.

I've noticed that people start to question who they are and what they want somewhere around their mid-30s to early 50s. Perhaps because it's a time where we have established a few things in life — a career, a relationship, some travel, a family, a home — and then there's a pause. 'So, what's next for me? This can't just be it, right? What about me?' And if we have some good people around us, these people might say — sure, you deserve some things for you, what do you want? And then…silence. Shit — I really don't know, and who am I anyway?

Sometimes it comes up around this age because we stop and have to pause/take a breath because we're just so damned tired. Tired of always looking after and focusing on others. Tired of always doing 'the right thing'. And it's not just psychologically tired but emotionally, mentally, and physically tired. It's not that we don't want to look after others, it's just that we want something for us too.

But then, what is that thing? What do I want? And even if I do happen to work it out, then how do I get it? How do I make it happen between everyone else's stuff that is going on — the basketball practices, playdates, cooking dinner, doing my work reports, being a presence on social media, attention for my partner, time with my children, making lunches, helping at the school, walking the dog, travelling to and from work, making origami flowers, having a shower for goodness sake! What chance do I have, even if I knew what I wanted and needed?

Finding You (Again)

So how do you find that voice, the one that tells you who you are, what you like, or what your opinion is?

I believe that perhaps it's first about discovering that you do have a voice, one that has not entirely disappeared but just got really quiet. And for you to hear it, you need to give yourself a chance to have some quiet so that you can find it. A great way to start to tap into this voice is to start asking yourself some questions. Not just any old questions but smart, quality questions. Ones that really start to open your mind up, that help you to find your inner voice, so that you may get back to who you really are.

Here are some great questions to ask yourself:

- What did I love to do when I was younger? What did I spend a lot of time doing?
- What do I watch, listen to, or do now that makes me feel happy?
- What will happen if I keep doing this for the next ten years?
- What is one thing that made me feel really good this past week?
- Who is someone I admire and why? What is one trait I admire that I could bring into my own life?
- If I could stop doing just one thing, what would it be? If I could start doing just one thing, what would it be?

Imagine you are 80 years old, looking back on your life — what do you wish you had done more of? What do you wish you had not worried about so much?

Once you find that voice again, your job is to keep checking in with yourself, and to keep listening. And listening doesn't just mean hearing. It means doing and acting on some of what it tells you. It means trying it out. This way you get some feedback about what your mind has told you, and then notice what fits and works for you, or what doesn't fit and work for you. Now, the more that you can do this, the more you will know and understand yourself. And the more you know and understand yourself, the better you can trust yourself.

You can learn to trust yourself in so many different ways.
- Trust that you know what is best for you.
- Trust that you have your own best interests and those around you at heart.
- Trust that only you can truly know when enough is enough, and when you need a change, a break, a shift. It is no-one else's job to do that or to know that. They actually cannot. It is physically impossible. No matter how well we think we know someone, or we think they know us, it is our responsibility to be the one to make the call on things. To say no, to choose how much is enough or too much, or when it is okay or not okay. No one else can possibly do this, or do it as well as you can — because they are not in your shoes. Only you know.
- Trust that you'll do the best you can with what you know.

It is so unfair to expect that others should know how we are, or should not ask us to do things because of x, y, and z, that they are crossing the boundaries/line. How can they? They are not us. They will not know, not ever. Even if we tell them, of course circumstances can change. So then sometimes it is okay or we want to, and sometimes not. We can't even tell ourselves sometimes. That's why it's crucial to check-in with yourself first. Then trust yourself.

Trust yourself that you will know what you need more than any other person on this planet. And trust that you are the only one who can determine this.

Then you must let others know (crazy I know!). They are not mind readers, and expecting them to know what we want or need is not only unfair but also such a burden for the other person to carry. Because how do we behave when the other person hasn't said, "It's okay honey, you're tired, I'll put the kids to bed/walk the dog"? What do we do? That's right, we get shitty and indignant and take it out on the other person. Do this enough times with someone who loves you and they start to panic and try to predict what will happen. We feel that they don't understand us and that we are being undermined. The other person carries the burden of constantly trying to predict needs and prevent fighting, and we carry the frustration, hurt and resentment of them trying to do it. Aaargh!

Okay, so once we start to really trust in ourselves and get our needs met, then the next part is to know that we can also trust ourselves to be okay. That is, that no matter what happens, we will cope, and we will be okay. This is something I see as the bottom line to a lot of anxiety. Imagine if you could say to yourself (and really believe it) that 'No matter what happens out there in the world, I will get through it. I will cope. I will be okay'. Imagine knowing that!

If you knew that you could cope with whatever life threw at you, imagine how much more peaceful you would feel. Now, when I say cope and be okay, I don't mean it won't hurt, or you won't be sad, or it won't take something to recover from, but bottom line, I mean you won't die. And really, this is where so much of our anxiety comes from. The survival response (fight-or-flight), which is all about 'not dying'. As long as the mind and body knows that it will not die, it is less likely to go into that panic/anxiety mode.

And this is a good thing! Because when you don't go into survival mode/anxiety state, then you are better able to think clearly and work out what you need to do. It's why our first responders are all trained to remain calm (even though they really should be highly anxious). Staying calm, knowing that they can trust themselves, knowing that they can cope with the situation will not only help them to not be anxious, but it will also help them to cope and get through the situation in the best possible way. They trust themselves — they trust in who they are, they trust what they know and their decisions, and doing this gets them through the crap. Trusting ourselves means knowing that we can cope with whatever gets thrown our way, which means checking in, listening, and acting on what that little voice is telling us.

REAL TALK

- Start to tune into your inner voice (no matter how small or quiet it has become) by asking yourself quality questions.
- Listen to these answers — and that means also take some action based on these answers.
- Check in with yourself — what is that like for me? Is this something that moves me forward in life? Does it make me happy? Does this 'feel' right for me?
- Building trust in yourself will help you to know that you can get through anything, and this helps to reduce stress and anxiety.

#7 LIVE A LIFE OF NO REGRETS

When I was 16, I got my first real boyfriend. It went something like this;

Him: 'Do you want to go out with me?'

Me: 'Well, I was going to but...' Then he kissed me. I thought, *'oh well, it can't hurt for a couple of weeks.'*

And that was it for about the next three or so years. By that point, I was going to university and thought that I needed to focus on my studies and believed that we were going in different directions. He was already working and living a different life, free of study.

Now, did I think it through that much at 19? No, but that's my adult interpretation of what happened. In reality, I think I just rounded it off saying that "I don't want to do this anymore, see ya!"

A few years later, I met back up with him at a friend's wedding, and the familiarity and comfort of our history and what I already knew about him and what he already knew about me was too tempting, and we got back together. This time we moved in together, and I was working in a corporate job, and he was…well, he was the same. Still drinking and partying like we were 16.

I was travelling a lot for work and making new friends and connections and enjoying a different lifestyle (again!). So, we started fighting and making each other miserable for quite a while there. I kept thinking — I should leave — but I kept coming back to this thought: 'No regrets'. I don't even know where it came from; it just seemed to be there and became (and still is) the motto for my life.

So I stayed with him until the life had been drained from the relationship, until I was completely sure that there was nothing left. The test for this is to ask myself — *when I'm 80 and sitting in my rocking chair reflecting on my life, will I regret not doing more or trying more?'* — if the answer is 'no', then I'm good to go (literally and figuratively). So when I finally got this answer, I then left him.

Inevitably, we were not on the same train; in fact, we were not even going to the same station. And if this was now, I would have realised that sooner, maybe immediately. But at the time, I did what I had to do, no regrets. Now I'm not suggesting that you stay with someone until the life drains from you both, but I do suggest that you check to see if you would have any regrets. What do you need to do or say to have no regrets?

I think that I may have adopted this motto one day after reading some research about people's regrets at the end of their lives. I read that people will more often regret the things they didn't do than the things they *did*. So I think that in that moment, I decided I would be someone who regretted what they did rather than someone who regretted what they didn't do. And in that moment I became the me who says yes to life — yes to new opportunities, having a go, trying new things, meeting new people, and yes, sometimes to fumbling and failing.

This attitude has led me to do and try the most amazing things. No regrets. Just say YES and see what happens. And I love that I have done this and continue to do this. These days I'm a little more discerning in what I choose as I now have some amazing tools to be able to powerfully choose things that really move my life forward in the direction I want to go and with the people who are most important to me.

And even now, I still sometimes defer to no regrets, but just not everything and anything like the good old days. I have no regrets living by the motto *no regrets*. Especially living this way when I was younger. It got me out of my box, it got me out of my comfort zone, it had me hang in there and explore and finish things to the end. Best decision ever!

And even today, looking back now (no, I'm not 80 yet, although I'm much closer to that end of the spectrum now), I am always so glad that I chose yes to each and every opportunity, that I kept going in some things that I wasn't too sure of, and that I have explored and lived this way for so long already. Even those things that I did do but that didn't work out or go the way I wanted or wished they had, I am so glad that I tried them and had a go. I am glad that I flogged that dead-end relationship with my ex-boyfriend because I can now sit here knowing that I gave it everything I had and that I never wondered, 'What if?'. I knew with all certainty that I had done everything I could and that it was the right way to go. No doubts, no regrets.

The 'what-ifs' — now that's a killer of peace right there. But because I implemented the no regrets motto, I was able to (for the most part) kill off the what-ifs. See, when you live by no regrets, there is no what-if haunting you. You just do and then know. Do and know. Don't and wonder. I will not die wondering. Not for the really important things, anyway. See, because I'll be left with just me at the end of this life. I'll only have to answer to me. And I know that I'm a pretty tough critic. I'm good at analysing. And so I do not want to be left with me at the end asking — what if? I want to be left with me at the end going — Woo hoo! What a life.

I remember a day, around ten years ago when I thought — *If I died now, I'd be okay with that.* Not because I actually wanted to die, but because I had already had such a fulfilled and amazing life, lived to the fullest, that I felt truly complete. Sometimes when I would share with people all the things I had done to that point, they would say, 'How can you be so young and have done so much? That's a full life right there'. And I would agree with them.

Little did I know that the next ten years were going to be even more amazing and that I would live and learn and do even more. I'm now married to the most gorgeous man, I have a beautiful daughter, I'm doing what I love in my work and business, and I live in an amazing part of the world amongst the trees and wildlife. And given that my life just gets better and better each decade, and that this is likely a function of saying yes and going for it, I can't wait for the next ten years — no regrets!

Side note: *No Regrets* does not mean No Pain. There has been heartache and difficult times from some of this, of course. But even with the pain and challenges that may have come from following this motto, it was all worthwhile. And it was worthwhile for a number of reasons, but mostly because, at the end of my life can I say to myself, and answer when I ask myself the question, 'Did you play full-out, were you on the playing field giving it your all?' Yes. 'Any what-ifs, any regrets?' — No. And then I can die peacefully, knowing that I gave it my all.

Now, what if you already have regrets? That you've already not done some things you wished you had. Making peace with things you wish you had done but didn't do — don't worry. There are still plenty of things that I wish I had done that I didn't do. Of course you can't do everything. But I make peace with it now. I choose to believe that everything has some learning opportunity in it — and I take what I need to learn from it, then let go of any attachment to it.

Some of the simplest words from the Ho'opo Prayer help establish a firm and loving attitude of 'No Regrets'. They can help move you forward in a whole-hearted way.

I am sorry. Please forgive me. Thank you. I love you.

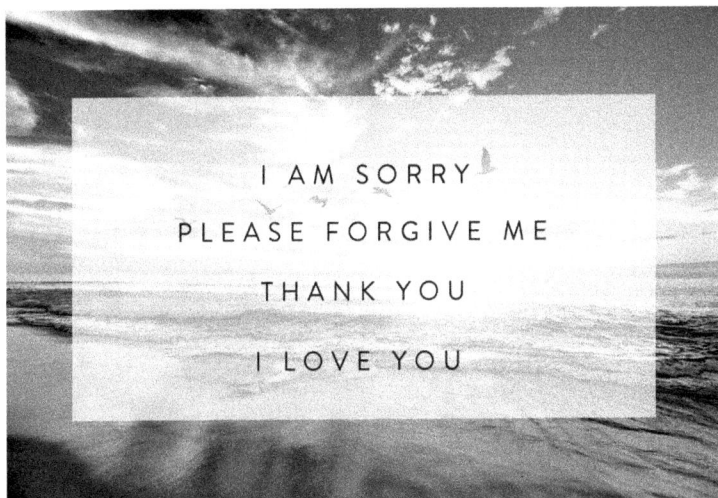

I AM SORRY

PLEASE FORGIVE ME

THANK YOU

I LOVE YOU

ABOUT THE AUTHOR

Dr Natasha Davison, affectionately referred to as *Dr Nat* by her clients, is a warm, friendly, kick-ass life coach and registered psychologist. With over 30 years' experience of personal and professional development and four university degrees, including a Doctorate in Psychology, Dr Nat is a highly sought after leading-edge professional.

Dr Nat is a speaker, trainer and author who works with coaches, clinicians, and high-achieving professionals who are committed to be the best they can be and are ready to clear any psychological blocks standing in their way. She is often described as a transformative coach and psychologist of the people, known for teaching "what works" and "keeping it real". Her workshops, talks and books are centered around her core ethos — *Real Talk, Real Change*, right now!

Dr Nat's education and training includes a Doctorate of Psychology, a Graduate Diploma of Education, a Postgraduate Diploma of Psychology, a Graduate Certificate of Education, Certificate IV Workplace Trainer & Assessor, a Bachelor of

Behavioural Science and multiple professional development trainings for life coaching including a Master Practitioner in NLP, Hypnosis and Timeline Therapy.

She is also extensively trained in multiple therapeutic modalities including Cognitive Behavioural Therapy (CBT), Gottman Method Couples Therapy, Motivational Interviewing (MI), and Acceptance and Commitment Therapy (ACT). Dr Nat holds a full registration with the governing body AHPRA and is a Member of the Australian Psychological Society (APS) and the College of Health Psychologists.

She is the owner of Your Local Psychologist clinic (yourlocalpsychologist.com.au) and has expanded her business to include eight fellow clinicians, equally dedicated to helping people be and feel their best every day.

Her latest book *Real Talk, Real Change* is a refreshing, easy-to-read, self-help book that helps anyone make real changes, real fast. Her candid and personal accounts, combined with her ability to help people recognise their own magnificence and rapidly harness their mindset, emotions and physiology towards greater living, is why Dr Nat is helping so many people become their BEST each year.

When not helping people, Dr Nat loves to spend time with her family and friends, play board and card games, learn new things, cook fresh produce from her home-grown veggie patch and walk her dog, Alfie. She loves to travel, attend awesome courses and read all the books she can possibly squeeze into her day.

For more information about Dr Nat's workshops and events please go to **drnatashadavison.com.au**.

TESTIMONIALS

Emotional to pragmatic. Natasha's gentle, inviting and caring approach shines through in our sessions. Natasha creates space for unhindered discussion; an open conversation with a professional that it feels as if I have known for years. Today, I confront my everyday situations with an enlivened sense of confidence. Confidence that was previously shadowed in doubt and anxiety. I am the best version of me I've ever known and I now have my very own 'Natasha voice' to guide me through my everyday challenges.

I just wanted to thank Natasha for all the hard work in helping me get to where I am today. Every day I use her wisdom to lead a better life.

Thanks to Natasha I now have strength, clarity and vision.

> **Robert S**

Natasha has done a wonderful job in helping me discover my 'whys'. I started off not knowing what I wanted in my life. I had no sense of direction though I thought I did.

I have been recently separated and felt like I was still struggling with relationships especially with my children and with myself. I wanted someone or something to fill that gap and make me feel complete. But I did not know that I had no purpose in life. I was just getting up, going to work and getting to bed every day and hoped life passes me by. I was struggling with no sense of purpose and no direction in life.

When I first met Natasha, I wanted to find a special someone because I felt it will make me happy. I thought I was happy and I wanted to share that with someone but she made me find my purpose through the whys. One week later, I realised what my purpose was, why I wanted what I wanted, what my visions were and where I wanted to be. I started with self-love. Within 8 weeks, I have found my true purpose in life, there are no doubts about what I want to achieve and what I want to create.

I haven't ever been this clear in my life and I must say Natasha has helped me to dig deep to reveal a part of me that was very dormant and afraid to shine.

My main goal started with self-love and moved into my career goals and I have reached 95% of my goals. The best part is that it has had a very positive effect in my relationship with my kids and my life. Natasha is a true professional. She listens, encourages and celebrates all my wins and reminds me that I need to celebrate my wins too. She has helped me through the challenges by providing tools and strategies to take with me in my life.

I want to thank Natasha for her coaching as I have made a total overhaul in my life for the better! In my world, Natatsha is one of my heroines that has taught me how to pick myself up in life's adversities and I am forever thankful.

Kokilla A

Before commencing coaching with Natasha, I was a little apprehensive as I did not understand the benefits associated with coaching, however I am now well and truly converted!

The coaching process with Natasha was thorough. We started with an initial consultation to set goals. Following this, we scheduled weekly sessions to ensure progress in achieving these goals was timely (I achieved my six-month goal in only two and a half months).

Via Natasha's sharing of skills and knowledge, I gained the tools needed to achieve success. As a direct result of Natasha's coaching, I have been able to adjust my thought process and modify behaviours to ensure positive results.

Natasha, thank you so much for your amazing energy, enthusiasm, guidance and professional expertise. Your coaching is the reason I have been able to achieve my goals and continue growing.

Kirsten S

Without your support and guidance, Nat, I wouldn't be kicking the goals I am now crushing. My self-worth would be buried somewhere, and I would still be questioning everything. But I'm not, because of you. Thank you, for guiding me, for pushing me, and for caring. My future world is now a ginormous great track of opportunities rather than paths of maybes. I love you for it, and I will never forget so much that you have taught me. You have helped me change inside, where it sticks. THANK YOU xx

Jennifer B

Natasha is an amazing coach and an even more amazing human being. Her powerful ability to help people is more than a gift.

When I started working with Natasha I was blown away by her knowledge and her expertise. She just knows how to ask the right questions and how to put you in the right direction. Doing coaching with Natasha definitely exceeded my expectations and I will always cherish our conversations. With her help I was able to achieve steady progress in my business and I was able to learn lots of lessons along the way. I would definitely recommend anyone who wants to achieve success in any area of life to work with Natasha. She's unstoppable!

Soly A

Coaching is something all should consider if you want to achieve more out of life. The experience of being coached by Natasha has been great. Natasha has the knack of being able to see through the bullshit I'm telling myself at times as to why I cannot achieve something. Her powerful questions, her insights continually cause me to think and allowed me to keep moving forward toward my goals. I feel good after each session knowing that I have achieved something or sorted in my mind how I need to go forward. My purpose and outcomes are a lot clearer. This took some time to work through because I knew what I wanted, but wasn't clear on what that looked like. Natasha's coaching certainly helped me work through this. Her questions caused me to reflect on stuff that was happening and look at things from a different angle, perspective. This helped immensely and enabled me to move forward and look at things which I once viewed as a negative in my life , as a gift instead. Very powerful!

Harry G

I was lucky enough to meet Dr Nat at a training course whilst she was writing her book. Something happened during that course that I will never forget. She excused herself from the group (and a training course she had paid money to be at) in order to take an out-of-hours call from a client that needed her. I was instantly blown away by her. I have never known a psychologist and coach who cared so deeply for their clients. I got to know Dr Nat and the more I knew about her, the more I discovered how incredibly gifted she is. She is without doubt one of the most incredible, dedicated, funny and deeply sincere persons that I have ever met. Her book is an absolute jewel. Every chapter spoke to me and gave me insight, understanding and even a laugh. It helped me through some personal difficulties and gave me real tools and strategies to move forward. Dr Nat is a gift to this world, and so is her book. Ten out of ten for both!

Christine W

Real Talk, Real Change – really changed me! This is one of the most practical, refreshing, 'real-life' books I have ever read. No psych jargon or babble attached. It just cuts straight through to workable solutions that you can immediately apply. I was blown away that a self-help book could be so personal, intimate and funny all at once. This will be staying on my book shelf for a long, long time.

Maureen V

When I read *Real Talk, Real Change*, my life was at a crossroad after going through a nasty divorce, losing my job and dealing with my Dad being diagnosed with dementia. After reading this book, I came to realise that it was OK to be sad about these things but also that the torment I was putting myself through was optional. After reading Dr Nat's own experiences, I realised I wasn't alone in how I felt. This book is in your face, but written with compassion at the same time! A great book that's easy to read with simple strategies — I loved it!

Melanie C

I absolutely loved *Real Talk, Real Change*. I connected with the book 100% and found it so easy to read, I couldn't put it down! I actually could hear Dr Nat talking while I was reading. It feels as though she is talking things through with you personally and helping you realise that what is going on is normal. I highly recommend this book, it has something valuable inside for everyone.

Zoe B

NATIONAL HELP LINES AND WEBSITES

Lifeline: 13 11 14, lifeline.org.au

Suicide Call Back Service:
1300 659467, suicidecallbackservice.org.au

Beyond Blue Support Service:
1300 22 4636, beyondblue.org.au

MensLine Australia: 1300 78 99 78, mensline.org.au
A telephone and online support, information and referral service, helping men to deal with relationship problems in a practical and effective way.

Kids Helpline: 1800 55 1800, kidshelpline.com.au
A free, private and confidential, telephone and online counselling service specifically for young people aged between 5 and 25.

QLife: 1800 184 527, qlife.org.au
QLife is Australia's first nationally-oriented counselling and referral service for LGBTI people.

Headspace: 1800 650 890, headspace.org.au
Free online and telephone service that supports young people aged between 12 and 25 and their families going through a tough time.

Black Dog Institute: blackdoginstitute.org.au
Information on symptoms, treatment and prevention of depression
and bipolar disorder.

SANE: 1800 187 263, www.sane.org
Information about mental illness, treatments, where to go for
support and help carers.

The Butterfly Foundation: 1800 4673, 8am–midnight (AEST)
Phone, webchat and email support for those experiencing an eating
disorder, friends, family, carers and professionals.

ReachOut: au.reachout.com
ReachOut is an online mental health organisation for young people
and their parents.

HealthInfoNet: healthinfonet.ecu.edu.au
Aboriginal and Torres Strait Islander health and wellbeing

Life in Mind:
02 4924 6900, lifeinmindaustralia.com.au/communities
Life in Mind is a national gateway connecting Australian suicide
prevention services to each other and the community.

Head to Health: headtohealth.gov.au
An innovative website that can help you find free and low-cost,
trusted online and phone mental health resources.

1800RESPECT: 1800 737 732, 1800respect.org.au
Confidential information, counselling and support service open 24
hours to support people impacted by sexual assault, domestic or
family violence and abuse.

Carers Australia: 1800 242 636, carersaustralia.com.au
Short-term counselling and emotional and psychological support
services for carers and their families in each state and territory.

Embrace Multicultural Mental Health:
embracementalhealth.org.au
A national platform for multicultural communities and Australian mental health services to access resources, services and information in a culturally accessible format.

MindSpot Clinic: 1800 61 44 34, mindspot.org.au
An online and telephone clinic providing free assessment and treatment services for Australian adults with anxiety or depression.

National Aboriginal Community Controlled Health Organisation (NACCHO): naccho.org.au
Aboriginal Community Controlled Health Services and Aboriginal Medical Services in each state and territory.

National Debt Helpline: 1800 007 007, ndh.org.au
Financial counselling is available from the National Debt Helpline. Financial counsellors are qualified professionals who provide information, advice and advocacy to people in financial difficulty. Their services are free, confidential, independent and non-judgmental.

Relationships Australia: 1300 364 277, relationships.org.au
A provider of relationship support services for individuals, families and communities.

Sometimes the bravest thing you can do is ask for help and be willing to let others help you. A whole new life can emerge from this brave place.
— Dr Nat

ACKNOWLEDGEMENTS

I would like to start by acknowledging my gorgeous husband, who has been and continues to be my greatest support and cheerleader. He provided me with the space and time to be able to make this book happen in the midst of our busy lives. Also to my beautiful daughter who went without her Mum at times so my attention could be on this book, my other baby.

To my mum and dad who shaped me into the person I am, someone who cares about other people and wants to help them. Thank you for providing me with the foundation of who I am, and my education and learning, so I could go on to do what I'm doing today.

To all of my family and friends — I acknowledge you for being a constant source of love and support, and for believing in me and what I do. You have all been there for me in your unique and different ways, all of you providing me with what I need at just the right time. Thank you — you rock!

I would like to acknowledge the Dean Publishing team, for being an ongoing source of "just the right amount" of whatever it was that I needed at the time. You are an awesome bunch of kind, generous and kick-ass people. A very special thank you to Natalie Deane, who was way more than an editor to me. Thank you for being such an unwavering and committed human being, and for never doubting me and that this was possible. You have a very special talent. I'd also like to acknowledge cartoonist Paul Joy whose incredible skill helped bring this book to life.

I would also like to acknowledge the hundreds of books and research papers I have read, the countless trainings, university courses, personal and professional development courses that I have attended, all of my many teachers, trainers, mentors, and coaches, and to life — for all of the crazy experiences you've thrown my way. All of this I gratefully acknowledge and know, that this has all brought me to where I am today.

ENDNOTES

1 Angelou, Maya (1969). *I Know Why the Caged Bird Sings*. New York: Random House.
2 Pocket Maya Angelou Wisdom: Inspirational quotes and wise words from a legendary icon, (Jan 2019), Hardie Grant London.
3 Watts, Alan. Audio. "The Story of the Chinese Farmer". Retrieved from YouTube August, 2020.
4 Maya Angelou. AZQuotes.com, Wind and Fly LTD, 2020. https://www.azquotes.com/quote/8498, accessed August 18, 2020.